Fodor's POCKET

washington,
D.C.

twelfth edition

Excerpted from *Fodor's Washington, D.C.*

fodor's travel publications
new york • toronto • london • sydney • auckland

www.fodors.com

contents

maps

on the road with fodor's

A TRIP TAKES YOU OUT OF YOURSELF. Concerns of life at home disappear, driven away by more immediate thoughts—about, say, what marvels will beguile the next day, or where you'll have dinner. That's where Fodor's comes in. We make sure that you know all your options in Washington, D.C., so that you don't miss something that's around the next bend just because you didn't know it was there. Mindful that the best memories of your trip might have nothing to do with what you came to see, we guide you to sights large and small. With Fodor's at your side, serendipitous discoveries are never far away.

Our success in showing you every corner of Washington, D.C. is a credit to our extraordinary writers. They're the kind of people you'd poll for travel advice if you knew them.

Susanna M. Carey, the freelance publications consultant and writer who updated Practical Information, divides her time between her clients and her 2½-year-old daughter, Charlotte. After living and working in and around Washington for more than 12 years, she has seen nearly every sight in the city and looks forward to gaining a new perspective through the eyes of a toddler.

Maureen Graney, a freelance editor and book producer who updated the Here and There chapter, regularly makes the rounds of Washington's top sights with her three young sons. The transplanted New Yorker loves her family's Capitol Hill town house.

Eating Out updater **Kristi Devlin** is a resident of Capitol Hill. Over the past year, she has executed over 70 wine and food tastings in D.C. restaurants, embassies, and hotels. She began her writing career as a news reporter and has recently written travel programs that have aired on PBS.

Our updater for the Where to Stay and Shopping chapters, **Robin Dougherty,** a native Washingtonian, recently moved back to D.C. after living in Miami and Boston. A longtime arts writer and former critic for the *Miami Herald*, she also writes a book column for the *Boston Globe*.

Karyn-Siobhan Robinson, who checked out the nightlife and arts scenes for this book, is a reporter, part-time actor, and essayist. She has lived in the Dupont Circle neighborhood since 1991 and is working on her first novel.

Don't Forget to Write

Your experiences—positive and negative—matter to us. If we have missed or misstated something, we want to hear about it. We follow up on all suggestions. Contact the *Pocket Washington, D.C.* editor at editors@fodors.com or c/o Fodor's at 1745 Broadway, New York, New York 10019. And have a fabulous trip!

Karen Cure

Karen Cure
Editorial Director

washington, d.c., area

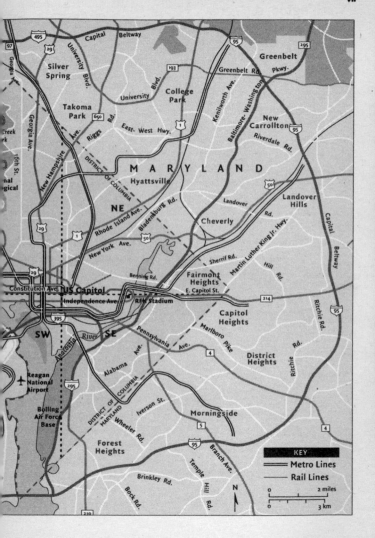

washington, d.c., metro system

Grosvenor-L
Strathmore
TO WHITE FLINT, TWINBROOK,
ROCKVILLE, AND SHADY GROVE

RED LINE

R
TO

Forest Glen

Medical Center

Bethesda

Friendship Heights

Tenleytown-AU

Van Ness-UDC

National
Zoological
Park

Cleveland Park

Woodley Park Zoo
Adams Morgan

Dupon
Circle

Far
No

MARYLAND

DISTRICT OF COLUMBIA

Court House

Rossyn

West Falls Church

Clarendon

McPherson Sq
Metro Cent
Federal Triang
Smithsoni

East Falls
Church

Virginia Sq

Ballston

L'Enfant

Arlington
Cemetery

Dunn Loring

ORANGE LINE
TO VIENNA

Pentagon

Pentagon City

Crystal
City

BLUE LINE

ational
Airport

V I R G I N I A

A L E X A N D R I A

Braddock Rd

King St

Van Dorn Street

Eisenhower
Avenue

BLUE LINE

Huntington

YELLOW LINE

Franconia-
Springfield

RED LINE
TO GLENMONT

Forest Glen

GREEN LINE
Greenbelt

Silver Spring

M A R Y L A N D

Takoma

College Park-
U of Md.

Prince George's
Plaza

MARYLAND
DISTRICT OF COLUMBIA

Georgia Ave-
Petworth

West Hyattsville

ORANGE LINE
New Carrollton

Van Ness-UDC

Fort Totten

National
Zoological
Park

Brookland-CUA

Landover

Columbia
Heights, Cardoza

lley Park Zoo
dams Morgan

U Street-
Shaw-Howard Univ

Rhode Island Ave

Dupont
Circle

Cleveland Ave

Cheverly

Farragut
North

Mt. Vernon
Sq.-UDC

New York Ave.

Deanwood

Gallery Pl-
Chinatown

Union Station

Minnesota Ave

McPherson Sq
Metro Center
Federal Triangle
Smithsonian

Archives-Navy Memorial

US Capitol

RFK Stadium

BLUE LINE

Capitol Heights

Addison Rd

L'Enfant Plaza

Eastern Market

Pentagon

Federal
Center
SW

Waterfront

Navy Yard

Anacostia

gon City
Crystal City

Congress Heights

DISTRICT OF COLUMBIA
MARYLAND

National
Airport

Naylor Road

LINE

Southern Ave.

Suitland

Braddock Rd

Branch Ave.

King St

GREEN LINE

Eisenhower
Avenue

N

0   4 miles

0   6 km

washington,
D.C.

In This Chapter

By Bruce Walker

introducing
washington, d.c.

WELCOME TO WASHINGTON. An ad for a local bank called Washington "the most important city in the world." It's the seat of our government, with some 300,000 federal employees. Our president lives here. Many of the 535 members of Congress who work here also live in the city. Washington is not known for its fashionably dressed inhabitants, nor its hip arts scene. The main business is politics, and that's probably what most people think of when they think about Washington: politicians, lobbyists, lawyers, public relations firms, government contractors.

So why come to Washington?

Let's start with its simple beauty. As you fly or drive to the city, one of the first things you might notice is its low profile: there are no skyscrapers. (The maximum allowable height of buildings is related to the width of the streets that run in front.) And that low profile makes Washington somehow seem more manageable as a tourist destination and a lot less overwhelming than a city where the buildings tower 40 or more stories overhead. Although a New York or Boston skyline is spectacular for its concentration of towering buildings, Washington is just as breathtaking for its open spaces and clean sight lines between some of its most famous attractions. It's almost like an amusement park, with all the best attractions concentrated in a relatively small area.

Washington does have one "skyscraper": the Washington Monument. Awe-inspiring in its own right, it also offers one of Washington's most impressive views—before you even go up to the top. Standing at the base the Washington Monument, you can see some of the most famous and familiar sights in the world. Look along the National Mall to the east and you'll see the Capitol, just 15 blocks away. Lining the Mall on both sides are many of the Smithsonian Institution's wonderful museums, as well as both buildings of the National Gallery of Art. To the north sits the White House. To the west are the Lincoln Memorial and the reflecting pool. Looking southward, you'll see the Jefferson Memorial and the cherry tree–lined Tidal Basin.

Washington isn't just the monuments and museums. There are first-class restaurants all around the city. Looking for some great ethnic food? Try Adams-Morgan. Looking for something on the fancy side? Try Georgetown or Downtown. Small parks all around the city function as seasonal flower pots, their beds replanted with new flowers as the seasons change. And D.C. has a flourishing arts scene: the Kennedy Center, with its full schedule of music and theater programs, is the jewel in Washington's performing arts crown. Arts programs thrive on a local and community level, too. Galleries abound in Georgetown and Dupont Circle.

One of the nicest things about Washington is how much you can do here for free. The national monuments, as well as many of the museums and parks, are free. A variety of festivals and concerts takes place throughout the year. During most evenings in the summer, the various military bands perform. The Smithsonian puts on a week-long Festival of American Folklife with loads of free entertainment. The National Symphony Orchestra performs on the Capitol lawn several times a year. And it's all free.

Visit Washington to remind yourself that the government does more than just take your money and engage in political

DAY THREE. Older children may enjoy morning tours of the Bureau of Engraving and Printing and the Capitol before heading off to the National Zoo. If you have younger children, start and end the day at the zoo. On cold or hot days, take advantage of the numerous indoor animal houses. If little ones wear out, you can rent strollers.

WASHINGTON IN FIVE DAYS WITH CHILDREN

DAYS ONE THROUGH THREE. Follow the three-day itinerary, *above.*

DAY FOUR. Start your fourth day at the Capital Children's Museum, where you can expect to spend at least three hours. If you and your children still have stamina, grab a bite to eat at Union Station on your way to the National Postal Museum. Older children may enjoy touring the International Spy Museum, followed by a trip to the Washington Navy Yard or Old Town Alexandria. With younger children, see creatures of the deep at the National Aquarium, followed by a trip to **GLEN ECHO PARK** for a play or puppet show.

In This Chapter

Updated by Maureen Graney

NW ◀ ▶ NE

Vermont Ave.

R St.

Logan Circle

Rhode Island Ave.

Florida Ave.

Q St.

R St.

Q St.

O St.

P St.

O St.

9th St.

New Jersey Ave.

3rd St.

1st St.

13th St.

12th St.

11th St.

10th St.

N St.

8th St.

7th St.

6th St.

5th St.

4th St.

N St.

New York Ave.

M St.

M St.

Massachusetts Ave.

L St.

New Jersey Ave.

North Capitol St.

3rd St.

Mt. Vernon Square

Massachusett Ave.

I St.

H St.

G St.

F St.

E St.

D St.

Old Downtown and Federal Triangle

2nd St.

I-395

Capitol Hill

Union Station
Columbus Memorial Fountain

Stanton Park

Pennsylvania Ave.

Constitution Ave.

Louisiana Ave.

D St.

Madison Dr.

National Gallery of Art

Smithsonian Institution

T H E   M A L L

Jefferson Dr.

National Air and Space Museum

US Capitol

NE

SE

E. Capitol St.

Independence Ave.

Maryland Ave.

C St.

Canal St.

The Mall

Folger Park

D St.

New Jersey Ave.

E St.

I-395

Southwest Fwy.

Virginia Ave.

G St.

G St.

Francis Case Memorial Br.

0   550 yards

0   500 meters

I St.

Washington Canal

N

SW ◀ ▶ SE

confluence of the Potomac and Anacostia rivers, not far from his estate at Mount Vernon. To give the young city a head start, Washington included the already thriving tobacco ports of Alexandria, Virginia, and Georgetown, Maryland, in the District of Columbia. In 1791, Pierre-Charles L'Enfant, a French engineer who had fought in the Revolution, created the classic plan for the city.

There's no denying that Washington, the world's first planned capital, is also one of its most beautiful. And though the federal government dominates many of the city's activities and buildings, there are places where you can leave politics behind. Washington is a city of vistas—pleasant views that shift and change from block to block, a marriage of geometry and art. Unlike other large cities, Washington isn't dominated by skyscrapers, largely because in 1910 Congress passed a height-restrictions act to prevent federal monuments from being overshadowed by commercial construction. Its buildings stretch out gracefully and are never far from expanses of green. Like its main industry, politics, Washington's design is a constantly changing kaleidoscope that invites contemplation from all angles.

THE MALL

The Mall is the heart of almost every visitor's trip to Washington. With nearly a dozen museums ringing the expanse of green, it's the closest thing the capital has to a theme park (unless you count the federal government itself, which has uncharitably been called "Disneyland on the Potomac"). As at a theme park, you may have to stand in an occasional line, but unlike the amusements at the real Disneyland, almost everything you'll see here is free. You may, however, need free, timed-entry tickets to some of the more popular traveling exhibitions. These are usually available at the museum information desk or by phone, for a service charge, from Ticketmaster (tel. 202/432–7328).

Of course, the Mall is more than just a front yard for these museums. Bounded on the north and south by Constitution and Independence avenues and on the east and west by 3rd and 14th streets, it's a picnicking park, a jogging path, an outdoor stage for festivals and fireworks, and America's town green. Nine of the Smithsonian Institution's 14 D.C. museums lie within these boundaries.

Sights to See

⑪ **ARTHUR M. SACKLER GALLERY.** When Charles Freer endowed the gallery that bears his name, he insisted on a few conditions: objects in the collection could not be loaned out, nor could objects from outside the collections be put on display. Because of the latter restriction it was necessary to build a second, complementary museum to house the Asian art collection of Arthur M. Sackler, a wealthy medical researcher and publisher who began collecting Asian art as a student in the 1940s. Sackler allowed Smithsonian curators to select 1,000 items from his ample collection and pledged $4 million toward the construction of the museum. The collection includes works from China, Southeast Asia, Korea, Tibet, and Japan. Articles in the permanent collection include Chinese ritual bronzes, jade ornaments from the 3rd millennium BC, Persian manuscripts, and Indian paintings in gold, silver, lapis lazuli, and malachite. The lower level connects to the Freer Gallery of Art. 1050 *Independence Ave. SW, The Mall, tel. 202/357–2700; 202/357–1729 TDD, www.asia.si.edu. Free. Daily 10–5:30. Metro: Smithsonian.*

☕ ⑨ **BUREAU OF ENGRAVING AND PRINTING.** The bureau turns out some 38-million dollars worth of currency a day. Paper money has been printed here since 1914, when the bureau relocated from the redbrick-towered Auditors Building at the corner of 14th Street and Independence Avenue. In addition to all the paper currency in the United States, stamps, military certificates, and presidential invitations are printed here, too. Tours usually last 35 minutes. *14th and C Sts. SW, The Mall, tel. 202/874–3188,*

the mall

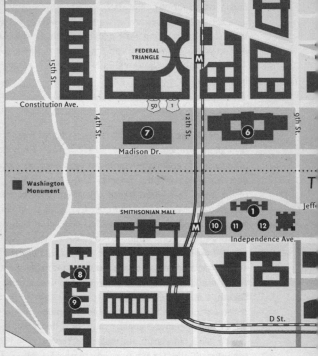

Arthur M. Sackler
Gallery, 11

Bureau of
Engraving and
Printing, 9

Freer Gallery
of Art, 10

Hirshhorn
Museum and
Sculpture
Garden, 2

National Air
and Space
Museum, 3

National Gallery
of Art, East
Building, 5

National Gallery
of Art,
West
Building, 4

National
Museum of
African Art, 12

National
Museum of
American
History, 7

National
Museum of
Natural
History, 6

Smithsonian
Institution
Building, 1

United States
Holocaust
Memorial
Museum, 8

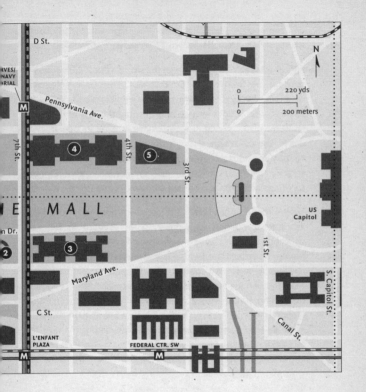

D St.

RVES/
NAVY
RIAL

Pennsylvania Ave.

M

7th St.

④

4th St.

⑤

3rd St.

N

0   220 yds

0   200 meters

US
Capitol

② E   **M A L L**

n Dr.

③

1st St.

S. Capitol St.

Maryland Ave.

C St.

Canal St.

L'ENFANT
PLAZA

M

FEDERAL CTR. SW

M

www.bep.treas.gov. Free. Sept.–May, weekdays 9–2; June–Aug., weekdays 9–2 and 5–6:30. Mar.–Sept., same-day timed-entry passes issued starting at 8 AM at Raoul Wallenberg Pl. SW entrance. Metro: Smithsonian.

⑩ FREER GALLERY OF ART. One of the world's finest collections of masterpieces from Asia, the Smithsonian's Freer Gallery of Art was made possible by an endowment from Detroit industrialist Charles L. Freer, who retired in 1900 and devoted the rest of his life to collecting art. Opened in 1923, four years after its benefactor's death, the collection, dating from Neolithic times to the 20th century, includes more than 27,000 works of art from the Far and Near East, including Asian porcelains, Japanese screens, Chinese paintings and bronzes, Korean stoneware, and Islamic objects.

Freer's friend James McNeill Whistler introduced him to Asian art, and the American painter is represented in the vast collection. On display is the Peacock Room, a blue-and-gold dining room decorated with painted leather, wood, and canvas. It was designed by Whistler for a British shipping magnate. Freer paid $30,000 for the entire room and moved it from London to the United States in 1904. The works of other American artists Freer felt were influenced by the Far East are also on display. A lower-level exhibition gallery connects the building to the Arthur M. Sackler Gallery. 12th St. and Jefferson Dr. SW, The Mall, tel. 202/357–2700; 202/357–1729 TDD, www.asia.si.edu. Free. Daily 10–5:30. Metro: Smithsonian.

② HIRSHHORN MUSEUM AND SCULPTURE GARDEN. A striking round building from 1974, the collection here includes some 12,000 works of art donated and bequeathed by Joseph H. Hirshhorn, a Latvian-born immigrant who made his fortune in this country running uranium mines. American artists such as Edward Hopper, Willem de Kooning, Andy Warhol, and Richard Diebenkorn are represented, as are modern European and Latin American masters, including Francis Bacon, Piet Mondrian, Jean Dubuffet, and Joan Miró.

The Hirshhorn's impressive sculpture collection is displayed throughout the museum, as well as on the lawns and granite surfaces of the fountain plaza and across Jefferson Drive in the sunken Sculpture Garden. Indoors and out, the display includes works by Henry Moore, Alexander Calder, and Alberto Giacometti. In the garden, Henri Matisse's *Backs I–IV* and Auguste Rodin's *Burghers of Calais* are highlights. Dubbed by detractors "the Doughnut on the Mall," the cylindrical, reinforced-concrete building designed by Pritzker Prize–winning architect Gordon Bunshaft is a fitting home for contemporary art. The grass and trees in the plaza, landscaped by James Urban, provide a soft backdrop for such work as Juan Munoz's *Conversation Piece*, an intriguing ensemble of five beanbag-like figures in bronze. *Independence Ave. and 7th St. SW, tel. 202/357–2700; 202/633–8043 TDD, www.hirshhorn.si.edu. Free. Museum daily 10–5:30, sculpture garden 7:30–dusk. Metro: Smithsonian or L'Enfant Plaza (Maryland Ave. exit).*

★ ☁ ❸ **NATIONAL AIR AND SPACE MUSEUM.** Opened in 1976, this museum attracts more than 9 million people each year. Its 23 galleries tell the story of aviation from the earliest human attempts at flight. Suspended from the ceiling like plastic models in a child's room are dozens of aircraft, including the *Wright 1903 Flyer*, which Wilbur Wright piloted over the sands of Kitty Hawk, North Carolina; Charles Lindbergh's *Spirit of St. Louis*; the X-1 rocket plane in which Chuck Yeager broke the sound barrier; and an X-15, the first aircraft to exceed Mach 6.

Other highlights include a backup model of the Skylab orbital workshop that you can walk through; the *Voyager*, which Dick Rutan and Jeana Yeager flew nonstop around the world; and the Lockheed Vega piloted by Amelia Earhart in 1932 in the first solo transatlantic flight by a woman. You can also see a piece of the moon: a 4-billion-year-old slice of rock collected by *Apollo* 17 astronauts. A permanent exhibition on the history of the scientific study of the universe is on the first floor.

Don't miss the museum's Lockheed Martin IMAX Theater, where educational films—some 3-D—are shown on the five-story-high screen. Purchase tickets up to two weeks in advance or as soon as you arrive (prices vary); then tour the museum. Upstairs, the Albert Einstein Planetarium is the first in the world to employ all-dome digital technology to create a feeling of movement through space. *Independence Ave. and 6th St. SW, tel. 202/357–1729; 202/357–1686 movie information; 202/357–1729 TDD, www.nasm.si.edu. Free, IMAX $7.50, planetarium $7.50. Daily 10–5:30. Metro: Smithsonian.*

★ ☺ ⑤ **NATIONAL GALLERY OF ART, EAST BUILDING.** The atrium is dominated by Alexander Calder's mobile *Untitled*, and the galleries display modern and contemporary art, though you'll also find major temporary exhibitions that span many years and artistic styles. Permanent works include Pablo Picasso's *The Lovers* and *Family of Saltimbanques*, four of Matisse's cutouts, Miró's *The Farm*, and Jackson Pollock's *Lavender Mist*.

The East Building opened in 1978 in response to the changing needs of the National Gallery. The trapezoidal shape of the building site, which had been taken up by tennis courts and rosebushes planted during Lady Bird Johnson's spruce-up campaign, prompted architect I. M. Pei's dramatic approach: two interlocking spaces shaped like triangles provide room for galleries, auditoriums, and administrative offices. Although the building's triangles contrast sharply with the symmetrical classical facade and gentle dome of the West Building, both structures are constructed of pink marble from the same Tennessee quarries. Despite its severe angularity, Pei's building is inviting. The axe-bladelike southwest corner has been darkened and polished smooth by thousands of hands irresistibly drawn to it.

To reach the East Building from the West Building, take the underground concourse, lined with gift shops, a café, and a cafeteria. But to appreciate Pei's impressive, angular East

Building, enter it from outside rather than from underground. Exit the West Building through its eastern doors, and cross 4th Street. (As you cross, look to the north: seeming to float above the Doric columns and pediment of the D.C. Superior Court are the green roof and redbrick pediment of the National Building Museum, four blocks away.) *Constitution Ave. between 3rd and 4th Sts. NW, tel. 202/737–4215; 202/842–6176 TDD, www.nga.gov. Free. Mon.–Sat. 10–5, Sun. 11–6. Metro: Archives/Navy Memorial.*

★ ❹ **NATIONAL GALLERY OF ART, WEST BUILDING.** The two buildings of the National Gallery hold one of the world's foremost collections of paintings, sculptures, and graphics. If you want to view the museum's holdings in (more or less) chronological order, it's best to start your exploration in the West Building. The rotunda, with its 24 marble columns surrounding a fountain topped with a statue of Mercury, sets the stage for the masterpieces on display in more than 100 galleries. A tape-recorded tour of the building's better-known holdings is available for a $5 rental fee on the main floor adjacent to the rotunda. If you'd rather explore on your own, get a map at one of the two art information desks; one is just inside the Mall entrance (off Madison Drive), and the other is near the Constitution Avenue entrance on the ground floor. The Micro Gallery, near the rotunda, offers computerized information on more than 1,700 works of art from the permanent collection. Touch-screen monitors provide access to color images, text, animation, and sounds to help you better understand—and appreciate—the works on display.

The National Gallery's permanent collection includes works from the 13th to 20th centuries. A comprehensive survey of Italian paintings and sculpture includes *The Adoration of the Magi*, by Fra Angelico and Filippo Lippi, and *Ginevra de'Benci*, the western hemisphere's only painting by Leonardo da Vinci. Flemish and Dutch works, displayed in paneled rooms, include *Daniel in the Lions' Den*, by Peter Paul Rubens, and a self-portrait by Rembrandt. The Chester Dale Collection comprises works by such Impressionists as Edgar Degas, Claude Monet, Auguste

Renoir, and Mary Cassatt. Salvador Dalí's *Last Supper* is also in this building.

The **National Gallery of Art Sculpture Garden** is between 7th and 9th streets along the Mall. Granite walkways take you through the garden, which is planted with shade trees, flowering trees, and perennials. Sculptures on display from the museum's permanent collection include Roy Lichtenstein's playful *House I*, Alexander Archipenko's *Woman Combing Her Hair*; Miró's *Personnage Gothique, Oiseau-Eclair*; and Isamu Noguchi's *Great Rock of Inner Seeking*. The huge central fountain is used as a skating rink during the winter.

Opened in 1941, the domed West Building was a gift to the nation from financier Andrew Mellon. (The dome was one of architect John Russell Pope's favorite devices. He designed the domed Jefferson Memorial and the National Archives, with its half-domed rotunda.) A wealthy financier and industrialist, Mellon served as secretary of the treasury under three presidents and as ambassador to the United Kingdom. He first came to D.C. in 1921 and lived for many years in a luxurious apartment near Dupont Circle, in a building that today houses the National Trust for Historic Preservation. Mellon had long collected great works of art, acquiring some on his frequent trips to Europe. In 1930 and 1931, when the Soviet government was short on cash and selling off many of its art treasures, Mellon bought more than $6 million worth of old masters, including Raphael's *The Alba Madonna* and Sandro Botticelli's *Adoration of the Magi*. Mellon promised his collection to America in 1936, the year before his death. He also donated the funds for the construction of the huge gallery and resisted suggestions it be named after him. *Constitution Ave. between 4th and 7th Sts. NW, The Mall, tel. 202/737–4215; 202/842–6176 TDD, www.nga.gov. Free. Mon.–Sat. 10–5, Sun. 11–6. Metro: Archives/Navy Memorial.*

(12) **NATIONAL MUSEUM OF AFRICAN ART.** Opened in 1987, this unique underground building houses galleries, a library,

photographic archives, and educational facilities. The museum's rotating exhibits present African visual arts, including sculpture, textiles, photography, archaeology, and modern art. Long-term installations explore the sculpture of sub-Saharan Africa, the art of Benin, pottery of Central Africa, the archaeology of the ancient Nubian city of Kerma, and the artistry of everyday objects. The museum's educational programs include films with contemporary perspectives on African life, storytelling programs, festivals, and hands-on workshops for families, all of which bring Africa's oral traditions, literature, and art to life. Workshops and demonstrations by African and African-American artists offer a chance to meet and talk to practicing artists. If you're traveling with children, look for the museum's free guide to the permanent "Images of Power and Identity" exhibition. *950 Independence Ave. SW, The Mall, tel. 202/ 357–2700; 202/357–1729 TDD, www.nmafa.si.edu. Free. Daily 10– 5:30. Metro: Smithsonian.*

🐾 ⑦ **NATIONAL MUSEUM OF AMERICAN HISTORY.** America's cultural, political, technical, and scientific past is explored at this museum. The incredible diversity of artifacts helps the Smithsonian live up to its nickname, "the Nation's attic." This is where you find Muhammad Ali's boxing gloves, Judy Garland's ruby slippers from *The Wizard of Oz*, and the Bunkers' living-room furniture from *All in the Family.*

Exhibits on the first floor emphasize the history of science and technology and include farm machines, automobiles, and a 280-ton steam locomotive. The permanent "Science in American Life" exhibit shows how science has shaped American life through such breakthroughs as the mass production of penicillin and the development of plastics. Another permanent exhibit looks at 19th-century life in three communities: industrial-age Bridgeport, Connecticut; the Jewish immigrant community in Cincinnati, Ohio; and African-Americans living in Charleston, South Carolina. The second floor is devoted to U.S. social and political history and has an exhibit on everyday American life just after the Revolution. A permanent exhibit,

"First Ladies: Political Role and Public Image," displays gowns worn by presidential wives, but it goes beyond fashion to explore the women behind the satin, lace, and brocade. The third floor has installations on money, musical instruments, and photography.

Be sure to check out Horatio Greenough's statue of the first president (near the west-wing escalators on the second floor). Commissioned by Congress in 1832, it was intended to grace the Capitol Rotunda. It was there for only a short while, however, since the toga-clad likeness proved shocking to legislators who grumbled that it looked as if the father of our country had just emerged from a bath. In the Hands on History Room, you can try some 30 activities, such as pedaling a high-wheeler bike or plucking an old stringed instrument. The Hands on Science Room has 25 experiments, including testing a water sample and exploring DNA fingerprinting. *Constitution Ave. and 14th St. NW, The Mall, tel. 202/357–2700; 202/357–1729 TDD, americanhistory.si.edu. Free. Daily 10–5:30; call for hrs of Hands on History and Hands on Science rooms. Metro: Smithsonian or Federal Triangle.*

★ ✋ ❻ **NATIONAL MUSEUM OF NATURAL HISTORY.** This is one of the great natural history museums in the world, filled with bones, fossils, stuffed animals, and other natural delights—124 million specimens in all. It was constructed in 1910, and two wings were added in the 1960s. The first-floor rotunda is dominated by a stuffed, 8-ton, 13-ft-tall African bull elephant, one of the largest ever found. (The tusks are fiberglass; the original ivory ones were far too heavy for the stuffed elephant to support.) Off to the right is the popular **Dinosaur Hall.** Fossilized skeletons here range from a 90-ft-long diplodocus to a tiny thescelosaurus neglectus (a small dinosaur so named because its disconnected bones sat for years in a college drawer before being reassembled).

Beyond the Dinosaur Hall is the permanent exhibit, **African Voices.** It shows the influence of Africa's peoples and culture with refreshingly up-to-date displays, including a Somali camel herder's portable house, re-creations of markets in Ghana (housewares, cola nuts, and yams are for sale), a Tunisian wedding tunic, and artifacts showing the Yoruba influence on Afro-Brazilian culture. The west wing, which houses displays of birds, mammals, and sea life, is closed for renovation through 2003. At the **Discovery Corner,** temporarily located outside the lobby of the IMAX theater, you can handle the elephant tusks, petrified wood, seashells, rocks, feathers, and other items on display.

The highlight of the second floor is the **Janet Annenberg Hooker Hall of Geology, Gems and Minerals.** Objects on display include a pair of Marie Antoinette's earrings, the Rosser Reeves ruby, spectacular crystals and minerals, and, of course, the Hope Diamond, a blue gem found in India and reputed to carry a curse (though Smithsonian guides are quick to pooh-pooh this notion). Also on the second floor is the **O. Orkin Insect Zoo** (named for the pest-control magnate who donated the money to modernize the exhibits), which has a walk-through rain forest. You can view at least 60 species of live insects, and there are tarantula feedings Tuesday through Friday at 10:30, 11:30, and 1:30.

The Samuel C. Johnson IMAX theater shows two- and three-dimensional natural-history films. The theater is also open Friday evenings from 6 for the "IMAX Jazz Café," an evening of live entertainment, food, and special IMAX films not shown during the day. Tickets for the theater can be purchased at the museum box office. *Constitution Ave. and 10th St. NW, tel. 202/ 357–2700; 202/357–1729 TDD, www.mnh.si.edu. Free; IMAX $7.50. Museum daily 10–5:30; Discovery Corner Tues.–Fri. noon–2:30, weekends 10:30–3:30; Discovery Corner passes distributed starting at 11:45 weekdays, 10:15 weekends. Metro: Smithsonian or Federal Triangle.*

❶ SMITHSONIAN INSTITUTION BUILDING. The first Smithsonian museum constructed, this red sandstone, Norman-style building is better known as the Castle. It was designed by James Renwick, the architect of St. Patrick's Cathedral in New York City. Although British scientist and founder James Smithson had never visited America, his will stipulated that should his nephew, Henry James Hungerford, die without an heir, Smithson's entire fortune would go to the United States, "to found at Washington, under the name of the Smithsonian Institution, an establishment for the increase and diffusion of knowledge." The museums on the Mall are the Smithsonian's most visible example of this ideal, but the organization also sponsors traveling exhibitions and maintains research posts in such outside-the-Beltway locales as the Chesapeake Bay and the tropics of Panama.

Smithson died in 1829, Hungerford in 1835, and in 1838 the United States received $515,169 worth of gold sovereigns. After eight years of congressional debate over the propriety of accepting funds from a citizen of another country, the Smithsonian Institution was finally established on August 10, 1846. The Castle building was completed in 1855 and originally housed all of the Smithsonian's operations, including the science and art collections, research laboratories, and living quarters for the institution's secretary and his family. The statue in front of the Castle's entrance is not of Smithson but of Joseph Henry, the scientist who served as the institution's first secretary. Smithson's body was brought to America in 1904 and is entombed in a small room to the left of the Castle's Mall entrance.

Today the Castle houses Smithsonian administrative offices as well as the **Smithsonian Information Center,** which can help you get your bearings and decide which attractions you want to visit. A 24-minute video provides an overview of the Smithsonian museums and the National Zoo, and monitors display information on the day's events. Interactive touch-screen displays provide more detailed information on the museums as well as other attractions in the capital. The center opens at 9 AM, an hour before the other museums, so you can plan your day without wasting valuable sightseeing time. 1000

Jefferson Dr. SW, The Mall, tel. 202/357–2700; 202/357–1729 TDD, www.si.edu. Free. Daily 9–5:30. Metro: Smithsonian.

★ ⑧ **UNITED STATES HOLOCAUST MEMORIAL MUSEUM.** Museums usually celebrate the best that humanity can achieve, but this James Ingo Freed–designed museum instead documents the worst. A permanent exhibition tells the stories of the millions of Jews, Gypsies, Jehovah's Witnesses, homosexuals, political prisoners, mentally ill, and others killed by the Nazis between 1933 and 1945. The graphic presentation is as extraordinary as the subject matter: upon arrival, you are issued an "identity card" containing biographical information on a real person from the Holocaust. The museum recounts the Holocaust with documentary films, video- and audiotaped oral histories, and a collection that includes such items as a freight car like those used to transport Jews from Warsaw to the Treblinka death camp, and the Star of David patches that Jewish prisoners were made to wear. Like the history it covers, the museum can be profoundly disturbing; it's not recommended for children under 11, although "Daniel's Story," in a ground-floor exhibit not requiring tickets, is designed for children ages 8 and up. The museum also has a multimedia learning center, a resource center for students and teachers, and a registry of Holocaust survivors. *100 Raoul Wallenberg Pl. SW (enter from Raoul Wallenberg Pl. or 14th St. SW), tel. 202/488–0400; 800/400–9373 tickets.com, www.ushmm.org. Free. Daily 10–5:30. Metro: Smithsonian.*

THE MONUMENTS

Washington is a city of monuments. In the middle of traffic circles, on tiny slivers of park, and at street corners and intersections, statues, plaques, and simple blocks of marble honor the generals, politicians, poets, and statesmen who helped shape the nation. The monuments dedicated to the most famous Americans are west of the Mall on ground reclaimed from the marshy flats of the Potomac. This is also the location of Washington's greatest single display of cherry trees, gifts from Japan.

the monuments

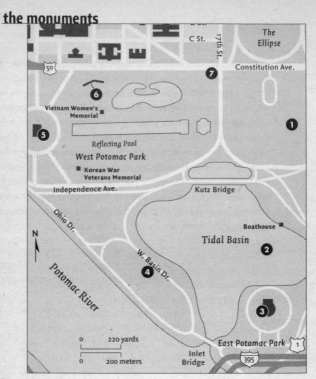

Sights to See

7 CONSTITUTION GARDENS. Many ideas were proposed to develop this 50-acre site. It once held "temporary" buildings erected by the navy before World War I and not removed until after World War II. President Nixon is said to have favored something resembling Copenhagen's Tivoli Gardens. The final design was a little plainer, with paths winding through groves of trees and, on the lake, a tiny island paying tribute to the signers of the Declaration of Independence, their signatures carved into a low stone wall. In 1986, President Reagan proclaimed the gardens a living legacy to the Constitution; in that spirit, a naturalization ceremony for new citizens now takes place here each year. *Constitution Ave. between 17th and 23rd Sts. NW, www.nps.gov/coga. Metro: Foggy Bottom.*

★ ☜ **4 FRANKLIN DELANO ROOSEVELT MEMORIAL.** This monument, designed by Lawrence Halprin, was unveiled in 1997. The 7½-acre memorial to the 32nd president employs waterfalls and reflection pools, four outdoor gallery rooms—one for each of his terms as president—and 10 bronze sculptures. The granite megaliths that connect the galleries are engraved with some of Roosevelt's most famous quotes, including, "The only thing we have to fear is fear itself." Although today the memorial is one of the most popular in the District, a delight to toddlers as well as to those who remember FDR firsthand, the FDR Memorial has had its share of controversy. Roosevelt is not portrayed with his omnipresent cigarette nor is he pictured in a wheelchair, which he used for the last 24 years of his life, after he contracted polio. However, a wheelchair that FDR used is now exhibited in the visitor center, and this D.C. memorial was the first purposely designed to be wheelchair accessible. It is also the first to honor a first lady; a bronze statue of Eleanor Roosevelt (without her trademark, a fur boa), stands in front of the United Nations symbol. *West side of Tidal Basin, The Mall, tel. 202/426–6841, www.nps.gov/fdrm. Free. 24 hrs; staffed daily 8 AM–midnight. Metro: Smithsonian.*

❸ JEFFERSON MEMORIAL. The monument honoring the third president of the United States incorporates his own architectural taste in its design. Jefferson had always admired the Pantheon in Rome—the rotundas he designed for the University of Virginia were inspired by its dome—so the memorial's architect, John Russell Pope, drew from the same source. In the 1930s Congress decided that Jefferson deserved a monument positioned as prominently as those in honor of Washington and Lincoln, so workmen scooped and moved tons of river bottom to create dry land on this spot directly south of the White House. Dedicated in 1943, it houses a statue of Jefferson, and its walls are lined with inscriptions based on the Declaration of Independence and his other writings. One of the best views of the White House can be seen from its top steps. *Tidal Basin, south bank, The Mall, tel. 202/426–6821, www.nps.gov/thje. Free. Daily 8 AM–midnight. Metro: Smithsonian.*

★ ❺ LINCOLN MEMORIAL. Nowadays many people consider the Lincoln Memorial the most inspiring monument in the city. This was not always the case. Although today it would be hard to imagine D.C. without the Lincoln and Jefferson memorials, both were criticized when first built. The Jefferson Memorial was dubbed "Jefferson's muffin"; critics lambasted the design as outdated and too similar to that of the Lincoln Memorial. Some also complained that the Jefferson Memorial blocked the view of the Potomac from the White House. Detractors of the Lincoln Memorial thought it inappropriate that the humble Lincoln be honored with what amounts to a modified but nonetheless rather grandiose Greek temple. The white Colorado-marble memorial was designed by Henry Bacon and completed in 1922. The 36 Doric columns represent the 36 states in the Union at the time of Lincoln's death; the names of the states appear on the frieze above the columns. Above the frieze are the names of the 48 states in the Union when the memorial was dedicated. (Alaska and Hawaii are represented with an inscription on the terrace leading up to the memorial.)

Daniel Chester French's somber statue of the seated president, in the center of the memorial, gazes out over the Reflecting Pool. Although the 19-ft-high sculpture looks as if it were cut from one huge block of stone, it's actually composed of 28 interlocking pieces of Georgia marble. (The memorial's original design called for a 10-ft-high sculpture, but experiments with models revealed that a statue that size would be lost in the cavernous space.) Inscribed on the south wall is the Gettysburg Address, and on the north wall is Lincoln's second inaugural address. Above each inscription is a mural painted by Jules Guerin: on the south wall is an angel of truth freeing a slave; the unity of North and South are depicted opposite. The memorial served as a fitting backdrop for Martin Luther King Jr.'s "I Have a Dream" speech in 1963.

Many visitors look only at the front and inside of the Lincoln Memorial, but there is much more to explore. On the lower level is the Lincoln Museum, a small exhibit financed with pennies collected by schoolchildren. There's also a set of windows that overlooks the huge structure's foundation. Stalactites (hanging from above) and stalagmites (rising from below) have formed underneath the marble tribute to Lincoln. Although visiting the area around the Lincoln Memorial during the day allows you to take in an impressive view of the Mall to the east, the best time to see the memorial itself is at night. Spotlights illuminate the outside, and inside light and shadows play across Lincoln's gentle face. *West end of Mall, The Mall, tel. 202/426–6895, www.nps.gov/linc. Free. 24 hrs; staffed daily 8 AM–midnight. Metro: Foggy Bottom.*

TIDAL BASIN. This placid pond was part of the Potomac until 1882, when portions of the river were filled in to improve navigation and create additional parkland, including the land upon which the Jefferson Memorial was later built. At the **boathouse** (tel. 202/479–2426), on the northeast bank of the Tidal Basin, you can rent paddleboats from mid-March through October, 10–6.

Two grotesque sculpted heads on the sides of the Inlet Bridge can be seen as you walk along the sidewalk that hugs the basin. The inside walls of the bridge also sport two other interesting sculptures: bronze, human-headed fish that spout water from their mouths. The bridge was refurbished in the 1980s at the same time the chief of the park—a Mr. Jack Fish—was retiring. Sculptor Constantine Sephralis played a little joke: these fish heads are actually Fish's head.

Once you cross the bridge, continue along the Tidal Basin to the right. This route is especially scenic when the cherry trees are in bloom. The first batch of these trees arrived from Japan in 1909. The trees were infected with insects and fungus, however, and the Department of Agriculture ordered them destroyed. A diplomatic crisis was averted when the United States politely asked the Japanese for another batch, and in 1912 Mrs. William Howard Taft planted the first tree. The second was planted by the wife of the Japanese ambassador, Viscountess Chinda. About 200 of the original trees still grow near the Tidal Basin.

The trees are now the centerpiece of Washington's Cherry Blossom Festival (www.nationalcherryblossomfestival.org), held each spring since 1935. The festivities are kicked off by the lighting of a ceremonial Japanese lantern that rests on the north shore of the Tidal Basin, not far from where the first tree was planted. The once-simple celebration has grown over the years to include concerts, martial-arts demonstrations, and a parade. Park-service experts try their best to predict exactly when the buds will pop. The trees are usually in bloom for about 10–12 days in late March or early April. When winter refuses to release its grip, the parade and festival are held anyway, without the presence of blossoms, no matter how inclement the weather. And when the weather complies and the blossoms are at their peak at the time of the festivities, Washington rejoices. *Bordered by Independence Ave. and Maine Ave., The Mall. Metro: Smithsonian.*

★ ⑥ **VIETNAM VETERANS MEMORIAL.** Renowned for its power to evoke poignant reflection, the Vietnam Veterans Memorial was conceived by Jan Scruggs, a former infantry corporal who had served in Vietnam. The stark design by Maya Lin, a 21-year-old Yale architecture student, was selected in a 1981 competition. Upon its completion in 1982, the memorial was decried by some veterans as a "black gash of shame." With the addition of Frederick Hart's realistic statue of three soldiers and a flagpole south of the wall, most critics were won over.

The wall is one of the most-visited sites in Washington, its black granite panels reflecting the sky, the trees, and the faces of those looking for the names of friends or relatives who died in the war. The names of more than 58,000 Americans are etched on the face of the memorial in the order of their deaths. Directories at the entrance and exit to the wall list the names in alphabetical order. For help in finding a name, ask a ranger at the blue-and-white hut near the entrance. Thousands of offerings are left at the wall each year: letters, flowers, medals, uniforms, snapshots. The National Park Service collects these and stores them in a warehouse in Lanham, Maryland, where they are fast becoming another memorial. Many visitors also bring paper and crayons or charcoal to make rubbings of the names of their loved ones. Tents are often set up near the wall by veterans groups; some provide information on soldiers who remain missing in action, and others are on call to help fellow vets and relatives deal with the sometimes overwhelming emotions that grip them when visiting the wall for the first time. *Constitution Gardens, 23rd St. and Constitution Ave. NW, The Mall, tel. 202/634–1568, www.nps.gov/vive. Free. 24 hrs; staffed daily 8 AM–midnight. Metro: Foggy Bottom.*

VIETNAM WOMEN'S MEMORIAL. After years of debate over its design and necessity, the Vietnam Women's Memorial, honoring the women who served in that conflict, was finally dedicated on Veterans' Day 1993. Sculptor Glenna Goodacre's stirring bronze group depicts two uniformed women caring for a wounded male soldier while a third woman kneels nearby. The eight trees around the plaza commemorate each of the women in the military who died in Vietnam. *Constitution Gardens, southeast of Vietnam Veterans Memorial, The Mall, www.nps.gov/vive/commem.htm. Metro: Foggy Bottom.*

★ ☾ ❶ **WASHINGTON MONUMENT.** At the western end of the Mall, the 555-ft, 5-inch Washington Monument punctuates the capital like a huge exclamation point. Visible from nearly everywhere in the city, it's truly a landmark.

In 1833, after years of quibbling in Congress, a private National Monument Society was formed to select a designer and to search for funds to construct this monument. Robert Mills's winning design called for a 600-ft-tall decorated obelisk rising from a circular colonnaded building. The building at the base was to be an American pantheon, adorned with statues of national heroes and a massive statue of Washington riding in a chariot pulled by snorting horses.

Because of the marshy conditions of L'Enfant's original site, the position of the monument was shifted to firmer ground 100 yards southeast. (If you walk a few steps north of the monument you can see the stone marker that denotes L'Enfant's original axis.) The cornerstone was laid in 1848 with the same Masonic trowel Washington himself had used to lay the Capitol's cornerstone 55 years earlier. The National Monument Society continued to raise funds after construction was begun, soliciting subscriptions of $1 from citizens across America. It also urged states, organizations, and foreign governments to contribute memorial stones for the construction. Problems arose in 1854, when members of the anti–Roman Catholic Know-Nothing party stole a block donated by Pope Pius IX, smashed it, and dumped its shards into the Potomac. This action, combined with a lack of funds, and the onset of the Civil War, kept the monument at a fraction of its final height, open at the top, and vulnerable to the rain. A clearly visible ring about a third of the way up the obelisk testifies to this unfortunate stage of the monument's history: although all of the marble in the obelisk came from the same Maryland quarry, the stone used for the second phase of construction came from a different stratum and is of a slightly different shade.

In 1876 Congress finally appropriated $200,000 to finish the monument, and the Army Corps of Engineers took over construction, thankfully simplifying Mills's original design. Work was finally completed in December 1884, when the monument was topped with a 7½-pound piece of aluminum, at that time one of the most expensive metals in the world. Four years later the monument was opened to visitors, who rode to the top in a steam-operated elevator. (Only men were allowed to take the 20-minute ride; it was thought too dangerous for women, who as a result had to walk up the stairs if they wanted to see the view.)

The view from the top takes in most of the District and parts of Maryland and Virginia. You are no longer permitted to climb the more than 800 steps leading to the top. (Incidents of vandalism and a number of heart attacks on the steps convinced the park service that letting people walk up on their own wasn't a good idea.)

The park service uses a free timed-ticket system. A limited number of tickets are available at the kiosk on 15th Street daily beginning half an hour before the monument opens, though in spring and summer lines start well before then. Tickets are good during a specified half-hour period. *Constitution Ave. and 15th St. NW, The Mall, tel. 202/426–6840; advance tickets (up to 6) 800/ 967–2283, www.nps.gov/wamo. Free; advance tickets require a $2 service and handling fee per ticket. Memorial Day–Labor Day, daily 8 AM–11:45 PM; Labor Day–Memorial Day, daily 9–4:45. Metro: Smithsonian.*

WEST POTOMAC PARK. Between the Potomac and the Tidal Basin, West Potomac Park is best known for its flowering cherry trees, which bloom only two weeks in late March or early April. During the rest of the year, West Potomac Park is just a nice place to relax, play ball, or admire the views at the Tidal Basin.

THE WHITE HOUSE AREA

In a world full of recognizable images, few are better known than the whitewashed, 32-room, Irish country house–like mansion at 1600 Pennsylvania Avenue. The residence of perhaps the single most powerful person on the planet, the White House has an awesome majesty, having been the home of every U.S. president but the father of our country, George Washington. This is where the buck stops in America and where the nation turns in times of crisis. After having a look at the White House, strike out into the surrounding streets to explore the president's neighborhood, which includes some of the city's oldest houses.

Sights to See

⑪ ART MUSEUM OF THE AMERICAS. Changing exhibits highlight 20th-century Latin American artists in this small gallery, part of the Organization of American States. The museum also screens documentaries on South and Central American art. A garden, open to the public, connects the Art Museum and the OAS building. *201 18th St. NW, White House area, tel. 202/458–6016, www.oas.org. Free. Tues.–Sun. 10–5. Metro: Farragut West.*

BLAIR HOUSE. A green canopy marks the entrance to Blair House, the residence used by heads of state visiting Washington. Harry S. Truman lived here from 1948 to 1952 while the White House was undergoing much-needed renovations. A plaque on the fence honors White House policeman Leslie Coffelt, who died in 1950 when Puerto Rican separatists attempted to assassinate President Truman at this site. The house is closed to the public. *1651 Pennsylvania Ave., White House area. Metro: McPherson Square.*

7 CORCORAN GALLERY OF ART. The Corcoran is Washington's largest non-federal art museum, as well as its first art museum. The beaux arts–style building, its copper roof green with age, was designed by Ernest Flagg and completed in 1897. The gallery's permanent collection of 14,000 works includes paintings by the greatest of the early American portraitists: John Copley, Gilbert Stuart, and Rembrandt Peale. The Hudson River School is represented by such works as *Mount Corcoran* by Albert Bierstadt and Frederic Church's *Niagara*. There are also portraits by John Singer Sargent, Thomas Eakins, and Mary Cassatt. The Walker Collection shows late-19th- and early 20th-century European paintings, including works by Gustave Courbet, Claude Monet, Camille Pissarro, and Pierre-Auguste Renoir. Dutch, Flemish, and French Romantic paintings are on display at the Clark Collection, as is the restored 18th-century Salon Doré of the Hotel de Clermont in Paris. Be sure to see Samuel Morse's *Old House of Representatives* and Hiram Powers's *Greek Slave*, which scandalized Victorian society. Photography and works by contemporary American artists are also among the Corcoran's strengths. The **Winder Building** (604 17th St., White House area), one block north, was erected in 1848 as one of the first office blocks in the capital. It served as the headquarters of the Union Army during the Civil War. *500 17th St. NW, White House area, tel. 202/ 639–1700, www.corcoran.org. $5 (free Mon. and Thurs. after 5). Mon., Wed., and Fri.–Sun. 10–5; Thurs. 10–9; tours of permanent collection Mon., Wed., and Fri. at noon; weekends at 10:30 AM, noon, and 2:30 PM; Thurs. at 7:30 PM. Metro: Farragut West or Farragut North.*

9 DAR MUSEUM. A beaux arts building serving as headquarters of the Daughters of the American Revolution, Memorial Continental Hall was the site of the DAR's annual congress until the larger Constitution Hall was built around the corner. An entrance on D Street leads to the DAR Museum. Its 33,000-item collection includes fine examples of colonial and federal furniture, textiles, quilts, silver, china, porcelain, stoneware, earthenware, and glass. Thirty-three period rooms are decorated in styles representative of various U.S. states, ranging from an 1850

the white house area

K St.

18th St.

FARRAGUT NORTH Ⓜ

17th St.

16th St.

Ⓜ FARRAGUT WEST

I St.

Ⓜ McPHERSON SQUARE

H St.

④

Pennsylvania Ave.

Jackson Pl.

③

Madison Pl.

15th St.

New York Ave.

⑤

G St.

Blair House

17th St.

⑥

②

The White House

E. Executive Ave.

⑭

G St.

F St.

F St.

14th St.

New York Ave.

⑦

E St.

Boy Scouts Memorial

Pennsylvania Ave. N.

⑬

Penna. Ave. S.

①

American Red Cross

⑧

D St.

⑨

⑫

C St.

Virginia Ave.

⑪ ⑩

Constitution Ave.

N

0   220 yards

0   200 meters

Art Museum of the Americas, 11

Corcoran Gallery of Art, 7

DAR Museum, 9

Department of the Interior, 8

Eisenhower Executive Office Building, 6

Ellipse, 12

Lafayette Square, 3

Organization of American States, 10

Pershing Park, 13

Renwick Gallery, 5

St. John's Episcopal Church, 4

Treasury Building, 14

White House, 2

White House Visitor Center, 1

California adobe parlor to a New Hampshire attic filled with toys from the 18th and 19th centuries. Two galleries—one of them permanent—hold decorative arts. Tours are available weekdays 10–2:30 and Sunday 1–5. During the "Colonial Adventure" tours, held the first and third Sundays of the month at 1:30 and 3 from September through May, costumed docents teach children ages five to seven about the exhibits and day-to-day life in colonial America. Make reservations at least 10 days in advance. *1776 D St. NW, White House area, tel. 202/879–3241, www.dar.org. Free. Weekdays 8:30–4, Sun. 1–5. Metro: Farragut West.*

8 **DEPARTMENT OF THE INTERIOR.** Designed by Waddy B. Wood, the Department of the Interior was the most modern government building in the city and the first large federal building with escalators and central air-conditioning when it was built in 1937. The outside of the building is somewhat plain, but inside, the hallways are lined with heroic oil paintings of dam construction, gold panning, and cattle drives. A guided tour takes you past more of the three dozen murals throughout the building. Reservations are required at least two weeks in advance for the tour.

Today the Department of the Interior oversees most federally owned land and natural resources. Exhibits in the museum outline the work of the Bureau of Land Management, the U.S. Geological Survey, the Bureau of Indian Affairs, the National Park Service, and other department branches. The Indian Craft Shop across the hall from the museum sells Native American pottery, dolls, carvings, jewelry, baskets, and books.

The **Department of the Interior Museum** (tel. 202/208–4743), on the first floor, displays more of its artwork holdings. You can enter the building at its E Street or C Street doors; adults must show photo ID. The small museum tells the story of the Department of the Interior, a huge agency dubbed "the Mother of Departments" because from it grew the Departments of Agriculture, Labor, Education, and Energy. The museum is open weekdays from 8:30 to 4:30, and the third Saturday of the month, from 1 to 4; admission is free. *C and E Sts. between 18th and 19th Sts. NW, White House area, www.doi.gov. Free. Metro: Farragut West.*

6 EISENHOWER EXECUTIVE OFFICE BUILDING. Once one of the most detested buildings in the city, the Eisenhower Executive Office Building (still called the Old Executive Office Building by locals) is now one of the most beloved. It was built between 1871 and 1888 as the State, War, and Navy Building, headquarters of those three executive-branch offices. Its architect, Alfred B. Mullett, styled it after the Louvre, but detractors quickly criticized the busy French Empire design—with a mansard roof, tall chimneys, and 900 freestanding columns—as an inappropriate counterpoint to the Greek Revival Treasury Building that sits on the other side of the White House. A 1930 plan was approved by Congress to replace the exterior in a Greek Revival style, but was shelved in 1933 due to the depressed economy. The granite edifice may look like a wedding cake, but its high ceilings and spacious offices make it popular with occupants, who include members of the executive branch. Nine presidents, including both Roosevelts, Richard Nixon, and George Bush have had offices here during their careers. The former office of the secretary of the navy, restored in the 1980s, shows the opulent style of that office at the turn of the 20th century; it has been an office for every vice president (except Hubert Humphrey) since Lyndon B. Johnson. *East side of 17th St., west of White House, White House area, tel. 202/395-5895. Tours have been suspended indefinitely; call ahead if you're planning a visit. Metro: Farragut West.*

12 ELLIPSE. From this expanse of lawn you can see the Washington Monument and the Jefferson Memorial to the south and the red-tile roof of the Department of Commerce to the east, with the tower of the Old Post Office sticking up above it. To the north you have a good view of the rear of the White House (the Ellipse was once part of its backyard); the rounded portico and Harry Truman's second-story porch are clearly visible. The White House's south lawn, also visible, is a heliport for *Marine One*, the president's helicopter. It's on the northern edge of the Ellipse that the National Christmas Tree is put up each year. In early December the president lights it during a festive ceremony that marks the official beginning of the holiday season. On spring and summer Wednesday evenings at 7, the U.S. Army holds a Twilight Tattoo of musical marching and gun salutes here.

The Ellipse's rather weather-beaten **gatehouse** (at the corner of Constitution Avenue and 17th Street) once stood on Capitol Hill. It was designed in 1828 by Charles Bulfinch, the first native-born American to serve as architect of the Capitol, and was moved here in 1874 after Frederick Law Olmsted redesigned the Capitol grounds. A twin of the gatehouse stands at Constitution Avenue and 15th Street. *Bounded by Constitution Ave. and E, 15th, and 17th Sts., White House area. Metro: Farragut West or McPherson Square.*

③ LAFAYETTE SQUARE. With such an important resident across the street, the National Capital Region's National Park Service gardeners lavish extra attention on this square's trees and flower beds. It's an intimate oasis amid downtown Washington.

When Pierre-Charles L'Enfant proposed the location for the Executive Mansion, the only building north of what is today Pennsylvania Avenue was the Pierce family farmhouse, which stood at the northeast corner of the present square. An apple orchard and a family burial ground were the area's two other features. During the construction of the White House, workers' huts and a brick kiln were set up, and soon residences began popping up around the square (though sheep would continue to graze on it for years). Soldiers camped in the square during the War of 1812 and the Civil War, turning it at both times into a muddy pit. Today, protesters set their placards up in Lafayette Square, jockeying for positions that face the White House. Although the National Park Service can't restrict the protesters' freedom of speech, it does try to limit the size of their signs.

In the center of the park—and dominating the square—is a large **statue of Andrew Jackson.** Erected in 1853 and cast from bronze cannons that Jackson captured during the War of 1812, this was the second equestrian statue made in America. (The first one, of King George III, was in New York City. Colonists melted it down for bullets during the Revolutionary War.) In the southeast corner is the park's namesake, the **Marquis de Lafayette,** the young French nobleman who came to America to fight in the Revolution.

The colonnaded building across Madison Place at the corner of Pennsylvania Avenue is an annex to the Treasury Department. The modern redbrick building farther on, at 717 Madison Place, houses judicial offices. Its design, with squared-off bay windows, is echoed in the taller building that rises behind it and in the **New Executive Office Building** on the other side of Lafayette Square. Planners in the '20s recommended that the private houses on Lafayette Square, many built in the federal period, be torn down and replaced with a collection of uniform neoclassical-style government buildings. A lack of funds providentially kept the neighborhood intact, and demolition was not even scheduled until 1957. In the early '60s Jacqueline Kennedy intervened and asked that the historic town houses and residential character be saved. A new plan devised by John Carl Warnecke set the large office buildings behind the historic row houses.

The next house down, yellow with a second-story ironwork balcony, was built in 1828 by Benjamin Ogle Tayloe. During the McKinley administration, Ohio senator Marcus Hanna lived here, and the president's frequent visits earned it the nickname the "Little White House." Dolley Madison lived in the next-door Cutts-Madison House after her husband died. Both the Tayloe and Madison houses are now part of the U.S. Court of Claims complex.

If you head east on H Street for half a block, you'll come to the **United States Government Bookstore** (1510 H St. NW, White House area, tel. 202/653-5075, www.gpo.gov/su_docs), the place to visit if you'd like to buy a few pounds of the millions of tons of paper the government churns out each year. Here is where you can find a copy of the latest federal budget or the *Surgeon General's Report on Nutrition and Health. Bounded by Pennsylvania Ave., Madison Pl., H St., and Jackson Pl., White House area. Metro: McPherson Square.*

⑩ ORGANIZATION OF AMERICAN STATES. The headquarters of the Organization of American States, which is made up of nations from North, South, and Central America, contains a patio adorned with a pre-Columbian–style fountain and lush tropical plants. This tiny rain forest is a good place to rest when Washington's summer heat is at its most oppressive. The upstairs Hall of the Americas contains busts of generals and statesmen from the 34 OAS member nations, as well as each country's flag. The OAS runs the Art Museum of the Americas. *17th St. and Constitution Ave. NW, White House area, tel. 202/458–3000, www.oas.org. Free. Weekdays 9–5:30. Metro: Farragut West.*

⑬ PERSHING PARK. A quiet sunken garden honors General John J. "Black Jack" Pershing, the first to hold the title General of the Armies, a rank congress created in 1919 to recognize his military achievements. Engravings on the stone walls recount pivotal campaigns from World War I, where Pershing commanded the American expeditionary force and conducted other military exploits. Ice-skaters glide on the square pool here in winter. *15th St. and Pennsylvania Ave., White House area. Metro: McPherson Square.*

⑤ RENWICK GALLERY. At the forefront of the crafts movement, the Renwick Gallery of the Smithsonian American Art Museum has a collection of exquisitely designed and made utilitarian items, as well as objects created out of such traditional crafts media as fiber and glass. The words "Dedicated to Art" are engraved above the entrance to the French Second Empire–style building, designed by architect James Renwick in 1859 to house the art collection of Washington merchant and banker William Wilson Corcoran. Corcoran was a Southern sympathizer who spent the duration of the Civil War in Europe. While he was away, the government pressed his unfinished building into service as a quartermaster general's post.

In 1871 the Corcoran, as it was then called, opened as the first private art museum in the city. Corcoran's collection quickly outgrew the building, and in 1897 it was moved to what's now the Corcoran Gallery of Art. After a stint as the U.S. Court of Claims, the building Renwick designed was restored, renamed after its architect, and opened in 1972 as the Smithsonian's Museum of American Crafts. Although crafts such as handwoven rugs and delicately carved tables were once considered less "artistic" than, say, oil paintings and sculptures, they have long since come into their own. The second-floor Grand Salon is still furnished in the opulent Victorian style Corcoran favored when his collection adorned its walls. *Pennsylvania Ave. at 17th St. NW, White House area, tel. 202/357–2531; 202/357–1729 TDD, www.americanart.si.edu. Free. Daily 10–5:30. Metro: Farragut West.*

4 ST. JOHN'S EPISCOPAL CHURCH. The golden-domed so-called Church of the Presidents sits across Lafayette Park from the White House. Every president since Madison has visited the church, and many worshiped here regularly. Built in 1816, the church was the second building on the square. Benjamin Latrobe, who worked on both the Capitol and the White House, designed it in the form of a Greek cross, with a flat dome and a lantern cupola. The church has been altered somewhat since then; additions include the Doric portico and the cupola tower. You can best sense the intent of Latrobe's design while standing inside under the saucer-shape dome of the original building. If you want to take a self-guided tour, brochures are available inside. *16th and H Sts. NW, Downtown, tel. 202/347–8766. Free. Weekdays 9–3; guided tours by appointment. Metro: McPherson Square.*

14 TREASURY BUILDING. Once used to store currency, this is the largest Greek Revival edifice in Washington. Robert Mills, the architect responsible for the Washington Monument and the Patent Office (now the Smithsonian American Art Museum), designed the grand colonnade that stretches down 15th Street. Construction of the Treasury Building started in 1836 and, after several additions, was finally completed in 1869. Its southern facade has a **statue of Alexander Hamilton,** the department's first secretary. The Andrew Johnson Suite was used by Johnson as the executive office while Mrs. Lincoln moved out of the White House. Other vestiges of its earlier days are the two-story marble Cash Room and a 19th-century burglarproof vault lining. *15th St. and Pennsylvania Ave. NW, White House area, tel. 202/622–0896; 202/622–0692 TDD. Tours have been suspended indefinitely; call ahead if you're planning a visit. Metro: McPherson Square or Metro Center.*

☝ ❷ **WHITE HOUSE.** This "house" surely has the best-known address in the United States: 1600 Pennsylvania Avenue. Pierre-Charles L'Enfant called it the President's House; it was known formally as the Executive Mansion; and in 1902 Congress officially proclaimed it the White House after long-standing common usage of that name. Irishman James Hoban's plan, based on the Georgian design of Leinster Hall in Dublin and of other Irish country houses, was selected in a 1792 contest. The building wasn't ready for its first occupant, John Adams, the second U.S. president, until 1800, and so George Washington, who seems to have slept everyplace else, never slept here. The building has undergone many structural changes since then. Andrew Jackson installed running water. James Garfield put in the first elevator. Between 1948 and 1952, Harry Truman had the entire structure gutted and restored, adding a second-story porch to the south portico. Each family that has called the White House home has left its imprint on the 132-room mansion. The most recent update is a running track installed for Bill Clinton.

In the past, selected public rooms on the ground floor and first floor had been open to visitors, but as of this writing, only certain organized groups are granted admission. The tour includes several rooms on the ground floor and, on the State Floor, the large white-and-gold **East Room,** the site of presidential social events. In 1814 Dolley Madison saved the room's full-length portrait of George Washington from torch-carrying British soldiers by cutting it from its frame, rolling it up, and spiriting it out of the White House. (No fool she, Dolley also rescued her own portrait.) One of Abraham Lincoln's sons once harnessed a pet goat to a chair and went for a ride through the East Room during a reception.

The federal-style **Green Room,** named for the moss-green watered silk that covers its walls, is used for informal receptions and "photo opportunities" with foreign heads of state. Notable furnishings here include a New England sofa that once belonged to Daniel Webster and portraits of Benjamin Franklin, John Quincy Adams, and Abigail Adams. The president and his guests are often shown on TV sitting in front of the Green Room's English Empire mantel, engaging in what are generally described as "frank and cordial" discussions.

The elliptical **Blue Room,** the most formal space in the White House, is furnished with a gilded Empire-style settee and chairs that were ordered by James Monroe. (Monroe asked for plain wooden chairs, but the furniture manufacturer thought such unadorned furnishings too simple for the White House and took it upon himself to supply chairs more in keeping with their surroundings.) The White House Christmas tree is placed in this room each year. (Another well-known elliptical room, the president's **Oval Office,** is in the West Wing of the White House, along with other executive offices.)

The **Red Room** is decorated as an American Empire–style parlor of the early 19th century, with furniture by the New York cabinetmaker Charles-Honoré Lannuier. The marble mantel is the twin of the one in the Green Room.

The **State Dining Room,** second in size only to the East Room, can seat 140 guests. It's dominated by G. P. A. Healy's portrait of Abraham Lincoln, painted after the president's death. The stone mantel is inscribed with a quote from one of John Adams's letters: "I pray heaven to bestow the best of blessings on this house and all that shall hereafter inhabit it. May none but honest and wise men ever rule under this roof." In Teddy Roosevelt's day a stuffed moose head hung over the mantel. *1600 Pennsylvania Ave. NW, Downtown, tel. 202/208–1631; 202/456–7041 (24-hr information line), www.whitehouse.gov. Metro: Federal Triangle.*

① WHITE HOUSE VISITOR CENTER. The visitor center is in charge of handing out White House tickets, but at this writing, tours of the White House are available only to children in grades 4 through 12, youth groups, and veterans groups. All tours must be arranged by a member of Congress, and they may be cancelled at any time without notice. Updates on the situation are available by calling the White House Visitor Office's 24-hour information line (tel. 202/456–7041). On display at the center are photographs, artifacts, and videos that relate to the White House's construction, decor, and residents. *Official address: 1450 Pennsylvania Ave. NW; entrance: Department of Commerce's Baldrige Hall, E St. between 14th and 15th Sts., White House area, tel. 202/208–1631 or 202/456–7041, www.nps.gov/whho. Free. Daily 7:30–4. Metro: Federal Triangle.*

CAPITOL HILL

The people who live and work on "the Hill" do so in the shadow of the edifice that lends the neighborhood its name: the gleaming white Capitol. More than just the center of government, however, the Hill also includes charming residential blocks lined with Victorian row houses and a fine assortment of restaurants, bars, and shops. Capitol Hill's precise boundaries are disputed: it's bordered to the west, north, and south by the Capitol, H Street NE, and I Street SE, respectively. Some argue that Capitol Hill extends east to the Anacostia River, others that it ends at 14th Street near Lincoln Park. The Capitol serves as the point from which the city is divided into quadrants: northwest, southwest, northeast, and southeast. North Capitol Street, which runs north from the Capitol, separates northeast

capitol hill

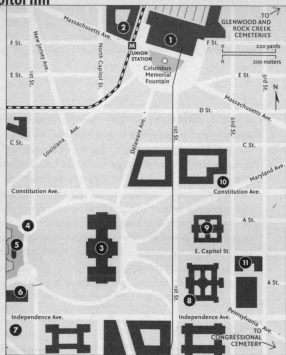

from northwest; East Capitol Street separates northeast and southeast; South Capitol Street separates southwest and southeast; and the Mall (Independence Avenue on the south and Constitution Avenue on the north) separates northwest from southwest.

Sights to See

❼ BARTHOLDI FOUNTAIN. Frédéric-Auguste Bartholdi, sculptor of the more famous—and much larger—Statue of Liberty, created this delightful fountain, some 30-ft tall, for the Philadelphia International Exposition of 1876. With its aquatic monsters, sea nymphs, tritons, and lighted globes (once gas, now electric), the fountain represents the elements of water and light. The U.S. Government purchased the fountain after the exposition and placed it on the grounds of the old Botanic Garden on the Mall. It was moved to its present location in 1932 and was restored in 1986. The surrounding Bartholdi Park—with its park benches and dense plantings—is a brown-bagger's delight at lunchtime. *1st St. and Independence Ave. SW, The Mall. Metro: Federal Center.*

★ ☙ **❸ CAPITOL.** As beautiful as the building itself are the Capitol grounds, landscaped in the late 19th century by Frederick Law Olmsted, who, along with Calvert Vaux, created New York City's Central Park. On these 68 acres are both the city's tamest squirrels and the highest concentration of TV news correspondents, jockeying for a good position in front of the Capitol for their "stand-ups." A few hundred feet northeast of the Capitol are two cast-iron car shelters, left from the days when horse-drawn trolleys served the Hill. Olmsted's six pinkish, bronze-top lamps directly east from the Capitol are worth a look, too.

The building's design was the result of a competition held in 1792; the winner was William Thornton, a physician and amateur architect from the West Indies. With its central rotunda and dome, Thornton's Capitol is reminiscent of Rome's

Pantheon, a similarity that must have delighted the nation's founders, who felt the American government was based on the principles of the Republic of Rome.

The cornerstone was laid by George Washington in a Masonic ceremony on September 18, 1793, and in November 1800, both the Senate and the House of Representatives moved down from Philadelphia to occupy the first completed section: the boxlike portion between the central rotunda and today's north wing. (Subsequent efforts to find the cornerstone Washington laid have been unsuccessful, though when the east front was extended in the 1950s, workers found a knee joint thought to be from a 500-pound ox that was roasted at the 1793 celebration.) By 1807 the House wing had been completed, just to the south of what's now the domed center, and a covered wooden walkway joined the two wings.

The "Congress House" grew slowly and suffered a grave setback on August 24, 1814, when British troops led by Sir George Cockburn marched on Washington and set fire to the Capitol, the White House, and numerous other government buildings. The wooden walkway was destroyed and the two wings gutted, but the walls were left standing after a violent rainstorm doused the flames. Fearful that Congress might leave Washington, residents raised money for a hastily built "Brick Capitol" that stood where the Supreme Court is today. Architect Benjamin Henry Latrobe supervised the rebuilding, adding such American touches as the corncob-and-tobacco-leaf capitals to columns in the east entrance of the Senate wing. He was followed by Boston-born Charles Bulfinch, and in 1826 the Capitol, its low wooden dome sheathed in copper, was finished.

North and south wings were added in the 1850s and '60s to accommodate a growing government trying to keep pace with a growing country. The elongated edifice extended farther north and south than Thornton had planned, and in 1855, to keep the scale correct, work began on a taller, cast-iron dome. President

Lincoln was criticized for continuing this expensive project while the country was in the throes of the Civil War, but he called the construction "a sign we intend the Union shall go on." This twin-shell dome, a marvel of 19th-century engineering, rises 285 ft above the ground and weighs 4,500 tons. It expands and contracts up to 4 inches a day, depending on the outside temperature. The allegorical figure atop the dome, often mistaken for Pocahontas, is called *Freedom*. Sculptor Thomas Crawford had first planned for the 19½-ft-tall bronze statue to wear the cloth liberty cap of a freed Roman slave, but Southern lawmakers, led by Jefferson Davis, objected. An "American" headdress composed of a star-encircled helmet surmounted with an eagle's head and feathers was substituted. A light just below the statue burns whenever Congress is in session.

The Capitol has continued to grow. In 1962 the east front was extended 33½ ft, creating 100 additional offices. Preservationists have fought to keep the west front from being extended, since it's the last remaining section of the Capitol's original facade. A compromise was reached in 1983, when it was agreed that the facade's crumbling sandstone blocks would simply be replaced with stronger limestone.

Tours of the Capitol start under the center of the **Rotunda's** dome. At the dome's center is Constantino Brumidi's 1865 fresco, *Apotheosis of Washington*. The figures in the inner circle represent the 13 original states; those in the outer ring symbolize arts, sciences, and industry. The flat, sculpture-style frieze around the Rotunda's rim depicts 400 years of American history and was started by Brumidi in 1877. While painting Penn's treaty with the Indians, the 74-year-old artist slipped on the 58-ft-high scaffold and almost fell off. Brumidi managed to hang on until help arrived, but he died a few months later from the shock of the incident. The work was continued by another Italian, Filippo Costaggini, but the frieze wasn't finished until American Allyn Cox added the final touches in 1953.

The Rotunda's eight immense oil paintings are of scenes from American history. The four scenes from the Revolutionary War are by John Trumbull, who served alongside George Washington and painted the first president from life. Twenty-nine people have lain in state or in honor in the Rotunda, including nine presidents, from Abraham Lincoln to Lyndon Baines Johnson. The most recently honored were the two U.S. Capitol policemen killed in the line of duty in 1998.

South of the Rotunda is **Statuary Hall**, once the legislative chamber of the House of Representatives. The room has an architectural quirk that maddened early legislators: a slight whisper uttered on one side of the hall can be heard on the other. (This parlor trick doesn't always work; sometimes the hall is just too noisy.) When the House moved out, Congress invited each state to send statues of two great deceased citizens for placement in the former chamber. Because the weight of the accumulated statues threatened to cave the floor in, some of the sculptures were dispersed to other spots in the Capitol.

To the north, on the Senate side, is the chamber once used by the Supreme Court and, above it, the splendid Old Senate Chamber (closed until further notice). In the Brumidi Corridor (also closed until further notice), on the ground floor of the Senate wing, frescoes and oil paintings of birds, plants, and American inventions adorn the walls and ceilings.

In 1981, Congress broke with tradition and moved the presidential swearing-in ceremony to the west side of the Capitol, which offers a dramatic view of the Mall and monuments below and can accommodate more guests than the east side, where most previous presidents took the oath of office.

Due to construction of the **Capitol Visitor Center,** a three-level subterranean education and information area beneath the east side of the building that is scheduled to open in 2005, tours begin on the west front of the Capitol in a special screening facility. They run Monday through Saturday from 9:30 AM to 3:30 PM. The free timed-entry tickets are distributed, one ticket per person, starting at 8:15 AM. Free gallery passes to watch the House or Senate in session can only be obtained from your senator or representative's office; both chambers are closed to the public when Congress is not in session. Note that there is a strict limit to the baggage and possessions that can be brought into the building: there are no facilities for checking personal belongings. If you're planning a visit, call ahead to check the status of tours and access; security measures may change. *East end of Mall, Capitol Hill, tel. 202/224–3121 Capitol switchboard; 202/225–6827 guide service, www.aoc.gov. Free. Metro: Capitol South or Union Station.*

CONGRESSIONAL CEMETERY. Established in 1807 "for all denomination of people," the Congressional Cemetery was the first national cemetery created by the government. Notables buried here include U.S. Capitol architect William Thornton, Marine Corps march composer John Philip Sousa, Civil War photographer Mathew Brady, and FBI director J. Edgar Hoover. There are also 76 members of Congress, many of them beneath ponderous markers. A brochure for a self-guided walking tour is available at the office. *1801 E St. SE, Capitol Hill, tel. 202/543–0539, www.congressionalcemetery.org. Daily dawn–dusk; office Mon.–Wed. and Fri. Metro: Stadium Armory or Potomac Ave.*

⑪ **FOLGER SHAKESPEARE LIBRARY.** The Folger Library's collection of works by and about Shakespeare and his times is second to none. The white-marble art deco building, designed by architect Paul Philippe Cret, is decorated with scenes from the Bard's plays. Inside, a gallery designed in the manner of an Elizabethan Great Hall, hosts rotating exhibits from the library's collection. *201 E. Capitol St. SE, Capitol Hill, tel. 202/544–7077, www.folger.edu. Free. Mon.–Sat. 10–4. Metro: Capitol South.*

⑤ **GRANT MEMORIAL.** The 252-ft-long memorial to the 18th American president and commander in chief of the Union forces during the Civil War is one of the largest sculpture groups in the city. The pedestal statue of Ulysses S. Grant on horseback displays his composure in the face of chaos. The soldiers and horses are notable for their realism; sculptor Henry Shrady spent 20 years researching and completing the memorial. *Near 1st St. and Maryland Ave. SW, Capitol Hill, The Mall. Metro: Federal Center.*

8 LIBRARY OF CONGRESS. One of the world's largest libraries, the Library of Congress contains some 115 million items, of which only a quarter are books. The remainder includes manuscripts, prints, films, photographs, sheet music, and the largest collection of maps in the world. Also part of the library is the Congressional Research Service, which, as the name implies, works on special projects for senators and representatives.

The copper-domed 1897's Thomas Jefferson Building is the oldest of the three buildings that make up the library. Like many other structures in Washington, the library was criticized when it was completed. Detractors felt its design, based on the Paris Opera House, was too florid. Congressmen were even heard to grumble that its dome—topped with the gilt "Flame of Knowledge"—competed with that of their Capitol. It's certainly decorative, with busts of Dante, Goethe, Nathaniel Hawthorne, and other great writers perched above its entryway. The *Court of Neptune*, Roland Hinton Perry's fountain at the base of the front steps, rivals some of Rome's best fountains.

Provisions for a library to serve members of Congress were originally made in 1800, when the government set aside $5,000 to purchase and house books that legislators might need to consult. This small collection was housed in the Capitol but was destroyed in 1814, when the British burned the city. Thomas Jefferson, then in retirement at Monticello, offered his personal library as a replacement, noting that "there is, in fact, no subject to which a Member of Congress may not have occasion to refer." Jefferson's collection of 6,487 books, for which Congress eventually paid him $23,950, laid the foundation for the great national library. (Sadly, another fire in 1851 destroyed two-thirds of Jefferson's books.) By the late 1800s it was clear that the Capitol could no longer contain the growing library, and the Jefferson Building was constructed. The **Adams Building,** on 2nd Street behind the Jefferson, was added in 1939. A third structure, the **James Madison Building,** opened in 1980; it's just south of the Jefferson Building, between Independence Avenue and C Street. Though not as architecturally interesting as the Jefferson building, evening literary readings and small exhibitions draw visitors here (exhibitions are open from 8:30 AM to 6 PM). The U.S. Copyright Office, in Room 401, is where all copyright registrations are issued.

The Jefferson Building opens into the Great Hall, richly adorned with mosaics, paintings, and curving marble stairways. The grand, octagonal Main Reading Room, its central desk surrounded by mahogany readers' tables under a 160-ft-high domed ceiling, is either inspiring or overwhelming to researchers. Computer terminals have replaced the wood card catalogs, but books are still retrieved and dispersed the same way: readers (18 years or older) hand request slips to librarians and wait patiently for their materials to be delivered. Researchers aren't allowed in the stacks, and only members of Congress and other special borrowers can check books out. Items from the library's collection—which includes one of only three perfect Gutenberg Bibles in the world—are on display in the Jefferson Building's second-floor Southwest Gallery and Pavilion. *Jefferson Bldg., 1st St. and Independence Ave. SE, tel. 202/707–4604, 202/707–5000, or 202/707–6400, www.loc.gov. Free. Mon.–Sat. 10 AM–5:30 PM; reading room hrs may extend later. Free tours Mon.–Sat. 10:30 AM, 11:30 AM, 1:30 PM, 2:30 PM and weekdays 3:30 PM. Metro: Capitol South.*

② **NATIONAL POSTAL MUSEUM.** The Smithsonian's priceless stamp collection, housed here, consists of a whopping 11 million stamps. Exhibits, underscoring the important part the mail has played in the development of America, include horse-drawn mail coaches, railway mail cars, airmail planes, and a collection of philatelic rarities. The National Museum of Natural History may have the Hope Diamond, but the National Postal Museum has the container used to mail the priceless gem to the Smithsonian. The family-oriented museum has more than 40 interactive and touch-screen exhibits. The museum takes up only a portion of what is the old Washington City Post Office, designed by Daniel Burnham and completed in 1914. Nostalgic odes to the noble mail carrier are inscribed on the exterior of the marble building. *2 Massachusetts Ave. NE, Capitol Hill, tel. 202/357–2700; 202/357–1729 TDD, www.si.edu/postal. Free. Daily 10–5:30. Metro: Union Station.*

4 PEACE MONUMENT. A white-marble memorial depicts America in the form of a woman grief-stricken over sailors lost at sea during the Civil War; she is weeping on the shoulder of a second female figure representing History. The plaque inscription refers movingly to Navy personnel who "fell in defence of the union and liberty of their country 1861–1865." *Traffic circle at 1st St. and Pennsylvania Ave. NW, The Mall. Metro: Union Station.*

ROCK CREEK CEMETERY. Rock Creek, the city's oldest cemetery, is administered by the city's oldest church, St. Paul's Episcopal, which erected its first building in 1712. (A single brick wall is all that remains of the original structure.) Many beautiful and imposing monuments are in the cemetery. The best known and most moving honors Marion Hooper "Clover" Adams, wife of historian Henry Adams; she committed suicide in 1885. Sculptor Augustus Saint-Gaudens created the enigmatic figure of a seated, shroud-draped woman, calling it *The Peace of God That Passeth Understanding*, though it's best known by the nickname "Grief." It may be the most moving sculpture in the city. *Rock Creek Church Rd. and Webster St. NW, Northeast, tel. 202/ 829–0585. Daily 7:30–dusk.*

10 SEWALL-BELMONT HOUSE. Built in 1800 by Robert Sewall, this is one of the oldest homes on Capitol Hill. Today it's the headquarters of the National Woman's Party. A museum inside chronicles the early days of the women's movement and the history of the house; there's also a library open to researchers by appointment. From 1801 to 1813 Secretary of the Treasury Albert Gallatin, who finalized the details of the Louisiana Purchase in his front-parlor office, lived here. This building was the only private house the British set fire to in Washington during their invasion of 1814, after a citizen fired on advancing British troops from an upper-story window (a fact later documented by the offending British general's sworn testimony, 30 years later, on behalf of the Sewalls in their attempt to secure war reparations from the U.S. government). This was, in fact, the only armed resistance the British met that day. The house is filled with period furniture and portraits and busts of such suffrage-movement leaders as Lucretia Mott, Elizabeth Cady Stanton, and Alice Paul, who wrote the Equal Rights Amendment in 1923. *144 Constitution Ave. NE, Capitol Hill, tel. 202/546–3989, www.sewallbelmont.org. Suggested donation $3. Tours on the hr Tues.–Fri. 11–3, Sat. noon–4. Metro: Union Station.*

9 SUPREME COURT BUILDING. It wasn't until 1935 that the Supreme Court got its own building: a white-marble temple with twin rows of Corinthian columns designed by Cass Gilbert. In 1800, the justices arrived in Washington along with the rest of the government but were for years shunted around various rooms in the Capitol; for a while they even met in a tavern. William Howard Taft, the only man to serve as both president and chief justice, was instrumental in getting the court a home of its own, though he died before it was completed.

The Supreme Court convenes on the first Monday in October and remains in session until it has heard all of its cases and handed down all of its decisions (usually the end of June). On Monday through Wednesday of two weeks in each month, the justices hear oral arguments in the velvet-swathed court chamber. Visitors who want to listen can choose to wait in either of two lines. One, the "three- to five-minute" line, shuttles you through, giving you a quick impression of the court at work. If you choose the other, and you'd like to stay for the whole show, it's best to be in line by 8:30 AM. The main hall of the Supreme Court is lined with busts of former chief justices; the courtroom itself is decorated with allegorical friezes. *1 1st St. NE, Capitol Hill, tel. 202/479–3000, www.supremecourtus.gov. Free. Weekdays 9–4:30. Metro: Union Station or Capitol South.*

❶ UNION STATION. With its 96-ft-high coffered ceiling gilded with 8 pounds of gold leaf, the city's train station is one of the capital's great spaces and is used for inaugural balls and other festive events. In 1902 the McMillan Commission—charged with suggesting ways to improve the appearance of the city— recommended that the many train lines that sliced through the capital share one main depot. Union Station was opened in 1908 and was the first building completed under the commission's plan. Chicago architect and commission member Daniel H. Burnham patterned the station after the Roman Baths of Diocletian.

For many coming to Washington, the capital city is first seen framed through the grand station's arched doorways. In its heyday, during World War II, more than 200,000 people swarmed through the building daily. By the '60s, however, the decline in train travel had turned the station into an expensive white-marble elephant. It was briefly, and unsuccessfully, transformed into a visitor center for the Bicentennial; but by 1981 rain was pouring in through its neglected roof, and passengers boarded trains at a ramshackle depot behind the station.

The Union Station you see today is the result of a restoration, completed in 1988, intended to begin a revival of Washington's east end. Between train travelers and visitors to the shops, restaurants, and a nine-screen movie theater, 70,000 people a day pass through the beaux arts building. The jewel of the structure is its main waiting room. Forty-six statues of Roman legionnaires, one for each state in the Union when the station was completed, ring the grand room. When the building was first opened, Pennsylvania Railroad president Alexander Cassatt (brother of artist Mary) ordered sculptor Louis Saint-Gaudens (brother of sculptor Augustus) to alter the statues, convinced that the legionnaires' skimpy outfits would upset female passengers. The sculptor obligingly added a shield to each figure, obscuring any offending body parts.

The east hall, now filled with vendors, is decorated with Pompeiian-style tracery and plaster walls and columns painted to look like marble. The station also has a secure presidential waiting room, now restored. This room was by no means frivolous: 20 years before Union Station was built, President Garfield was assassinated in the public waiting room of the old Baltimore and Potomac terminal on 6th Street.

The **Columbus Memorial Fountain,** designed by Lorado Taft, sits in the plaza in front of Union Station. A caped, steely eyed Christopher Columbus stares into the distance, flanked by a hoary, bearded figure (the Old World) and an Indian brave (the New). *Massachusetts Ave., north of Capitol, tel. 202/289–1908, www.unionstationdc.com. Metro: Union Station.*

☙ ➏ **UNITED STATES BOTANIC GARDEN.** This glistening, plant-filled oasis, established by Congress in 1820, is the oldest botanic garden in North America. The recently renovated Palm House conservatory is the center of attention. Now called the Jungle, it houses rainforest plants and includes walkways 24 ft above ground. With equal attention paid to science and aesthetics, the Botanic Garden contains plants from all around the world with an emphasis on tropical and economically useful plants, desert plants, and orchids. On a three-acre plot immediately to the west, the new **National Garden** is scheduled to open in 2004. *1st St. and Maryland Ave. SW, Downtown, tel. 202/225–8333, www.usbg.gov. Free. Daily 10–5. Metro: Federal Center SW.*

OLD DOWNTOWN AND FEDERAL TRIANGLE

Just because Washington is a planned city doesn't mean the plan was executed flawlessly. Pierre-Charles L'Enfant's design has been alternately shelved and rediscovered several times in the past 200 years. Nowhere have the city's imperfections been more visible than on L'Enfant's grand thoroughfare, Pennsylvania Avenue. By the early '60s it had become a national disgrace; the dilapidated buildings that lined it were pawn shops and cheap souvenir stores. While riding up Pennsylvania Avenue in his inaugural parade, a disgusted John F. Kennedy is said to have turned to an aide and said, "Fix it!" Washington's downtown—once within the diamond formed by Massachusetts, Louisiana, Pennsylvania, and New York avenues—had its problems, too, many the result of riots that rocked the capital in 1968 after the assassination of Martin Luther King Jr. In their wake, many businesses left the area and moved north of the White House.

In recent years developers have rediscovered "old downtown," and buildings are now being torn down or remodeled at an amazing pace. After several false starts, Pennsylvania Avenue is shining once again. This walk explores the old downtown section of the city, then swings around to check the progress on the monumental street that links the Capitol with the President's House. (Note: where E Street meets Pennsylvania Avenue, the intersection creates an odd one-block stretch that looks like Pennsylvania Avenue but is technically E Street. Buildings usually choose to associate themselves with the more prestigious-sounding "Pennsylvania Avenue" rather than "E Street.")

Sights to See

⓰ **APEX BUILDING.** The triangular Apex Building, completed in 1938, is the home of the Federal Trade Commission. The relief decorations over the doorways on the Constitution Avenue side depict agriculture (the harvesting of grain, by Concetta

Scaravaglione) and trade (two men bartering over an ivory tusk, by Carl Schmitz). Michael Lantz's two heroic statues, on either side of the rounded eastern portico, each depict a muscular, shirtless workman wrestling with a wild horse and represent man controlling trade. Just across 6th Street is a three-tier fountain decorated with the signs of the zodiac; it's a memorial to Andrew Mellon, who, as secretary of the treasury, oversaw construction of the $125 million Federal Triangle. (A deep-pocketed philanthropist, Mellon was the driving force behind the National Gallery of Art, just across Constitution Avenue.) *7th St. and Pennsylvania Ave. NW, Downtown. Metro: Archives/Navy Memorial.*

④ **CHINATOWN.** If you don't notice you're entering Washington's compact Chinatown by the Chinese characters on the street signs, the ornate, 75-ft-wide **Friendship Arch** spanning H Street might clue you in. Though Chinatown's main cross-streets may appear somewhat down-at-the-heels, this area borders many blocks undergoing revitalization, and it's still the place to go for Chinese food in the District. Cantonese, Szechuan, Hunan, and Mongolian are among the delectable culinary styles you'll find here. Nearly every restaurant has a roast duck hanging in the window, and the shops here sell Chinese goods. Most interesting are traditional pharmacies purveying folk medicines such as dried eels, powdered bones, and unusual herbs for teas and broths believed to promote health, longevity, and sexual potency. *Bounded by G, H, 5th, and 8th Sts., Downtown. Metro: Gallery Place/Chinatown.*

CITY MUSEUM. The beautiful beaux arts Carnegie Library building, once Washington's Central Public Library, has undergone a spectacular renovation and is scheduled to open in 2003. It will be the only museum devoted to the nation's capital. Run by the Historical Society of Washington, D.C., the facility will include a library reading room, an archaeology exhibit, and galleries for multimedia presentations about Washington's neighborhoods, ethnic groups, and prehistory. The museum is across the street from the new Washington Convention Center. The Historical

old downtown and federal triangle

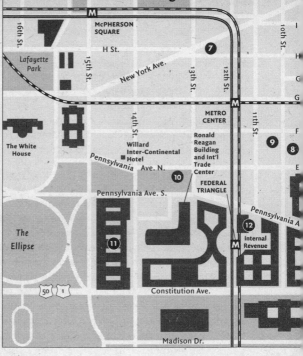

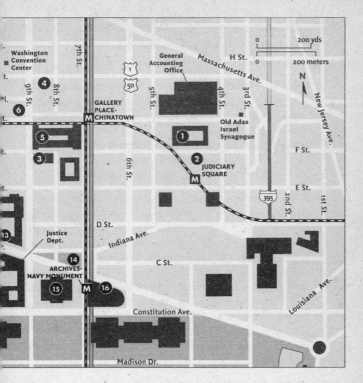

Washington
Convention
Center

7th St.

9th St.
8th St.

GALLERY
PLACE-
CHINATOWN

General
Accounting
Office

H St.

Massachusetts Ave.

5th St.
4th St.
3rd St.

New Jersey Ave.

Old Adas
Israel
Synagogue

F St.

6th St.

JUDICIARY
SQUARE

E St.

395

2nd St.
1st St.

D St.

Justice
Dept.

Indiana Ave.

C St.

ARCHIVES-
NAVY MONUMENT

Louisiana Ave.

Constitution Ave.

Madison Dr.

0   200 yds
0   200 meters
N

Society's offices, currently at Heurich House, will move here. 801 K St. NW, tel. 202/785–2068, www.hswdc.org. Call for admission fee. Call to confirm opening date and to check hrs. Metro: Gallery Place/Chinatown or Mt. Vernon Square/UDC.

FEDERAL TRIANGLE. To the south of Freedom Plaza, Federal Triangle consists of a mass of government buildings constructed between 1929 and 1938. Notable are the Department of Commerce (with the National Aquarium inside), the District Building, the Old Post Office, the Internal Revenue Service Building, the Department of Justice, the National Archives, and the Apex Building, which houses the Federal Trade Commission.

Before Federal Triangle was developed, government workers were scattered throughout the city, largely in rented offices. Looking for a place to consolidate this workforce, city planners hit on the area south of Pennsylvania Avenue known, at the time, as "Murder Bay," a notorious collection of rooming houses, taverns, tattoo parlors, and brothels. A uniform classical architectural style, with Italianate red-tile roofs and interior plazas reminiscent of the Louvre, was chosen for the building project. Federal Triangle's planners envisioned interior courts filled with plazas and parks, but the needs of the motorcar foiled any such grand plans. 15th St. and Pennsylvania and Constitution Aves., Downtown. Metro: Federal Triangle.

⑧ FORD'S THEATRE. In 1859, Baltimore theater impresario John T. Ford leased the First Baptist Church building that stood on this site and turned it into a successful music hall. The building burned down late in 1863, and Ford built a new structure on the same spot. The events of April 14, 1865, would shock the nation and close the theater. On that night, during a performance of *Our American Cousin*, John Wilkes Booth entered the state box and assassinated Abraham Lincoln. The stricken president was carried across the street to the house of tailor William Petersen. Charles Augustus Leale, a 23-year-old surgeon, was the first man to attend to the president. To let Lincoln know that someone was nearby, Leale held his hand throughout the night. Lincoln died the next morning.

The federal government bought Ford's Theatre in 1866 for $100,000 and converted it into office space. It was remodeled as a Lincoln museum in 1932 and was restored to its 1865 appearance in 1968. The basement museum—with artifacts such as Booth's pistol and the clothes Lincoln was wearing when he was shot—reopened in 1990. The theater itself continues to present a complete schedule of plays; *A Christmas Carol* is an annual holiday favorite. *511 10th St. NW, Downtown, tel. 202/426–6924, www.nps.gov/foth. Free. Daily 9–5; theater closed to visitors during rehearsals and matinees (generally Thurs. and weekends); Lincoln museum in basement remains open at these times. Metro: Metro Center or Gallery Place.*

⑩ FREEDOM PLAZA. Western Plaza was renamed Freedom Plaza in honor of Martin Luther King Jr. in 1988. Its east end is dominated by a statue of General Casimir Pulaski, the Polish nobleman who led an American cavalry corps during the Revolutionary War and was mortally wounded in 1779 at the Siege of Savannah. He gazes over a plaza inlaid with a detail from L'Enfant's original 1791 plan for the Federal City. Bronze outlines the President's Palace and the Congress House; the Mall is represented by a green lawn. Cut into the edges are quotations about the capital city, not all of them complimentary. To compare L'Enfant's vision with today's reality, stand in the middle of the map's Pennsylvania Avenue and look west. L'Enfant had planned an unbroken vista from the Capitol to the White House, but the Treasury Building, begun in 1836, ruined the view. Turning to the east, you'll see the U.S. Capitol sitting on Jenkins Hill like an American Taj Mahal. *Bounded by 13th, 14th, and E Sts. and Pennsylvania Ave., Downtown. Metro: Federal Triangle.*

❸ INTERNATIONAL SPY MUSEUM. Cryptologists, masters of disguise, and former officials of the CIA, FBI, and KGB are among the advisors of this museum, which displays the largest collection of spy artifacts anywhere in the world. Fittingly, it's just a block away from FBI headquarters. Fans of John Le Carré can revel in exhibits such as the School for Spies, which describes what makes a good spy and how they are trained; War of the Spies, devoted to sophisticated Cold War spy techniques; and 21st-Century Spying, in which espionage experts analyze the latest spy trends. 800 F St. NW, Downtown, tel. 202/393–7798, www.spymuseum.org. $11. Apr.–Oct., daily 10–8; Nov.–Mar., daily 10–6. Metro: Gallery Place/Chinatown.

🖑 ⑬ **J. EDGAR HOOVER FEDERAL BUREAU OF INVESTIGATION BUILDING.** Tours of the FBI Building's interior have been suspended indefinitely at this writing. The hulking structure, opened in 1974, has been decried from birth as hideous. Even Hoover himself is said to have called it the "ugliest building I've ever seen." Those hoping for a dose of espionage history can walk a block to the new International Spy Museum. 10th St. and Pennsylvania Ave. NW (enter on E St. between 9th and 10th Sts. for tours), Downtown, tel. 202/324–3447, www.fbi.gov. Metro: Federal Triangle or Gallery Place/Chinatown.

⑥ **MARTIN LUTHER KING JR. MEMORIAL LIBRARY.** The only D.C. building designed by Mies van der Rohe, one of the founders of modern architecture, this squat black building at 9th and G streets is the largest public library in the city. A mural on the first floor depicts events in the life of the Nobel Prize–winning civil rights activist. Used books are almost always on sale at bargain prices in the library's gift shop. 901 G St. NW, Downtown, tel. 202/727–1111. Free. Mon.–Thurs. 10–9, Fri. and Sat. 10–5:30, Sun. 1–5. Metro: Gallery Place/Chinatown.

🖑 **MCI CENTER.** The Washington Wizards, Washington Mystics, and Georgetown Hoyas play basketball here, and the Washington Capitals call it home during hockey season. This is also the site of concerts and shows—including ice-skating extravaganzas and the circus. 601 F St. NW (between 6th and 7th Sts.), Downtown, tel. 202/628–3200 MCI Center; 202/432–7328 Ticketmaster. Metro: Gallery Place/Chinatown.

⑪ NATIONAL AQUARIUM. The western base of Federal Triangle between 14th and 15th streets is the home of the Department of Commerce, charged with promoting U.S. economic development and technological advancement. When it opened in 1932 it was the world's largest government office building. It's a good thing there's plenty of space; incongruously, the National Aquarium is housed inside. Established in 1873, it's the country's oldest public aquarium, with more than 1,200 fish and other creatures—such as eels, sharks, and alligators—representing 270 species of fresh-and saltwater life. The exhibits look somewhat dated, but the easy-to-view tanks, accessible touching pool (with crabs and sea urchins), low admission fee, and general lack of crowds make this a good, low-key outing with children. *14th St. and Constitution Ave. NW, Downtown, tel. 202/482–2825, www.nationalaquarium.com. $3. Daily 9–5 (last admission at 4:30); sharks fed Mon., Wed., and Sat. at 2; piranhas fed Tues., Thurs., and Sun. at 2; alligators fed Fri. at 2. Metro: Federal Triangle.*

⑮ NATIONAL ARCHIVES. If the Smithsonian Institution is the nation's attic, the Archives is the nation's basement, and it bears responsibility for important government documents and other items. The Declaration of Independence, the Constitution, and the Bill of Rights are on display in the building's rotunda, in a case made of bulletproof glass, equipped with green filters and filled with helium gas (to protect the irreplaceable documents). At night and on Christmas—the only day the Archives is closed—the cases and documents are lowered into a vault. Other objects in the Archives' vast collection include bureaucratic correspondence, veterans and immigration records, treaties, Richard Nixon's resignation letter, and the rifle Lee Harvey Oswald used to assassinate John F. Kennedy.

The Archives fills the area between 7th and 9th streets and Pennsylvania and Constitution avenues on Federal Triangle. Beside it is a small park with a modest memorial to Franklin Roosevelt. The desk-size piece of marble on the sliver of grass is exactly what the president asked for (though this hasn't stopped fans of the 32nd president from building a grand memorial at the Tidal Basin). Designed by John Russell Pope, the Archives was erected in 1935 on the site of the old Center Market. This large block had been a center of commerce since the early 1800s. At that time, barges were unloaded here, when Constitution Avenue was still the City Canal. A vestige of this mercantile past lives on in the name given to the two semicircular developments across Pennsylvania Avenue from the Archives—Market Square. Residential development continues to further enliven this stretch of Pennsylvania Avenue.

Head to the Constitution Avenue side of the Archives. All the sculpture that adorns the building was carved on the site, including the two statues that flank the flight of steps facing the Mall, *Heritage* and *Guardianship*, by James Earle Fraser. Fraser also carved the scene on the pediment, which represents the transfer of historic documents to the recorder of the Archives. (Like nearly all pediment decorations in Washington, this one bristles with electric wires designed to thwart the advances of destructive starlings.) Call at least three weeks in advance to arrange a behind-the-scenes tour. *Constitution Ave. between 7th and 9th Sts. NW, Downtown, tel. 202/501–5000; 202/501–5205 tours, www.nara.gov. Free. Apr.–Labor Day, daily 10–9; Labor Day–Mar., daily 10–5:30; tours weekdays at 10:15 and 1:15. Metro: Archives/Navy Memorial.*

❶ NATIONAL BUILDING MUSEUM. The open interior of this mammoth redbrick edifice is one of the city's great spaces and has been the site of inaugural balls for more than 100 years. (The first ball was for Grover Cleveland in 1885; because the building wasn't finished at the time, a temporary wooden roof and floor were erected.) The eight central Corinthian columns are among the largest in the world, rising to a height of 75 ft. Although they look like marble, each is made of 70,000 bricks, covered with plaster and painted to resemble Siena marble. For years, this breathtaking hall has been the setting for the annual *Christmas in Washington* TV special.

Formerly known as the Pension Building, it was erected between 1882 and 1887 to house workers who processed the pension claims of veterans and their survivors, an activity that intensified after the Civil War. The architect was U.S. Army Corps of Engineers general Montgomery C. Meigs, who took as his inspiration Rome's Palazzo Farnese. The museum is devoted to architecture and the building arts, with recent exhibits on office design, the many uses of wood, and the designs of Disney theme parks. There are also some hands-on displays here that are great for kids.

Before entering the building, walk down its F Street side. The terra-cotta frieze by Caspar Buberl between the first and second floors depicts soldiers marching and sailing in an endless procession around the building. Architect Meigs lost his eldest son in the Civil War, and, though the frieze depicts Union troops, he intended it as a memorial to all who were killed in the bloody war. Meigs designed the Pension Building with workers' comfort in mind. Note the three "missing" bricks under each window that helped keep the building cool by allowing air to circulate. Tours are offered at 12:30 Monday through Wednesday; 11:30, 12:30, 1:30 Thursday through Saturday; and 12:30 and 1:30 Sunday. Family programs are available at 2:30 Saturdays and Sundays. 401 F St. NW, between 4th and 5th Sts., tel. 202/272–2448, www.nbm.org. Free. Mon.–Sat. 10–5, Sun. 11–5. Metro: Judiciary Square.

② NATIONAL LAW ENFORCEMENT OFFICERS MEMORIAL. The National Law Enforcement Officers Memorial is a 3-ft-high wall that bears the names of more than 15,000 American police officers killed in the line of duty since 1792. On the third line of panel 13W are the names of six officers killed by William Bonney, better known as Billy the Kid. J. D. Tippit, the Dallas policeman killed by Lee Harvey Oswald, is honored on the ninth line of panel 63E. Given the dangerous nature of police work, more names are added to the memorial each year. (Some of the most recent additions include the names of the 71 officers who died in the terror attacks of 2001.) Two blocks from the memorial is a visitor center with exhibits on its history. Computers there allow you to look up officers by name, date of death, state, and department. A small shop sells souvenirs. Call to arrange for a free tour. *605 E St. NW, Downtown, tel. 202/737–3400, www.nleomf.com. Free. Weekdays 9–5, Sat. 10–5, Sun. noon–5. Metro: Chinatown/Gallery Place.*

❼ NATIONAL MUSEUM OF WOMEN IN THE ARTS. Works by female artists from the Renaissance to the present are showcased at this museum, which opened its permanent collection in 1987. The beautifully restored 1907 Renaissance Revival building was designed by Waddy B. Wood; ironically, it was once a Masonic temple, for men only. In addition to displaying traveling shows, the museum has a permanent collection that includes paintings, drawings, sculpture, prints, and photographs by Georgia O'Keeffe, Mary Cassatt, Élisabeth Vigée-Lebrun, Frida Kahlo, and Camille Claudel. *1250 New York Ave. NW, Downtown, tel. 202/783–5000, www.nmwa.org. $8. Mon.–Sat. 10–5, Sun. noon–5. Metro: Metro Center.*

NATIONAL PORTRAIT GALLERY. This museum is in the Old Patent Office Building along with the Smithsonian American Art Museum. Unfortunately, a major renovation of the building, set to last through 2005, means that the gallery is closed. *8th and F Sts. NW, Downtown, tel. 202/357–2700; 202/357–1729 TDD, www.npg.si.edu. Closed during renovation. Metro: Gallery Place/Chinatown.*

NATIONAL THEATRE. Except for brief periods spent as a movie house, the National Theatre has been mounting plays in this location since 1835. Helen Hayes saw her first play here at the age of six; she then vowed to become an actress. If you plan ahead, you can take a free tour that includes the house, stage, backstage, wardrobe room, dressing rooms, the area under the stage, the Helen Hayes Lounge, and the memorabilia-filled archives. Tours are given for a minimum of 10 people, and only when there is no show; make reservations at least two weeks in advance. *1321 Pennsylvania Ave. NW (intersection of 13th and E Sts.),*

Downtown, tel. 202/783–3370, www.nationaltheatre.org. Free. Metro: Metro Center.

⑭ NAVY MEMORIAL. A huge outdoor plaza, this memorial includes a granite map of the world and a 7-ft statue, *The Lone Sailor*. In summer, military bands perform on its concert stage. Next to the memorial, in the Market Square East Building, is the Naval Heritage Center, which has a gift shop and the Navy Log Room, where you can use computers to look up the service records of navy veterans. The 242-seat, wide-screen Arleigh & Roberta Burke Theater shows a rotating series of historical sea service movies at noon. A memorial to General Winfield Scott Hancock, whose forces repelled Pickett's Charge at Gettysburg, is in the park adjacent to the Navy Memorial. *701 Pennsylvania Ave. NW, tel. 202/737–2300, www.lonesailor.org. Films free. Naval Heritage Center Mar.–Nov., Mon.–Sat. 9:30–5. Metro: Archives/Navy Memorial.*

OLD ADAS ISRAEL SYNAGOGUE. This is the oldest synagogue in Washington. Built in 1876 at 6th and G streets NW, the redbrick federal Revival–style building was moved to its present location in 1969 to make way for an office building. Exhibits in the Lillian and Albert Small Jewish Museum inside explore Jewish life in Washington. *701 3rd St. NW, tel. 202/789–0900. Suggested donation $3. Museum Sun.–Thurs. noon–4. Metro: Judiciary Square.*

⑤ OLD PATENT OFFICE BUILDING. The two Smithsonian museums that share the Old Patent Office Building's space are closed through 2005 because of its renovation. The National Portrait Gallery, which has presidential portraits, *Time* magazine covers, and Civil War photographs, paintings, and prints, is on the south side. The Smithsonian American Art Museum, with displays on Early American and western art, is on the north.

Construction of the south wing, designed by Washington Monument architect Robert Mills, started in 1836. When the huge Greek Revival quadrangle was completed in 1867 it was the largest building in the country. Many of its rooms housed glass display cabinets filled with the scale models that were required to accompany patent applications.

During the Civil War, the Patent Office, like many other buildings in the city, was turned into a hospital. Among those caring for the wounded here were Clara Barton and Walt Whitman. In the 1950s the building was threatened with demolition to make way for a parking lot, but the efforts of preservationists saved it. *G St. between 7th and 9th Sts., Downtown, www.nps.gov.opot. Metro: Gallery Place/Chinatown.*

OLD POST OFFICE. When it was completed in 1899, this Romanesque structure on Federal Triangle was the largest government building in the District, the first with a clock tower, and the first with an electric power plant. Despite these innovations, it earned the sobriquet "old" after only 15 years, when a new District post office was constructed near Union Station. When urban planners in the '20s decided to impose a uniform design on Federal Triangle, the Old Post Office was slated for demolition. The fanciful granite building was saved first because of a lack of money during the Depression, then thanks to the intercession of preservationists. Major renovation was begun in 1978, and in 1983 the Old Post Office Pavilion—an assortment of shops and restaurants inside the airy central courtyard—opened.

Park service rangers who work at the Old Post Office consider the observation deck in the clock tower one of Washington's best-kept secrets. Although not as tall as the Washington Monument, it offers nearly as impressive a view. Even better, it's usually not as crowded, the windows are bigger, and—unlike the monument's windows—they're open, allowing cool breezes to waft through. (For self-guided tours, use the entrance at 12th Street and Pennsylvania Avenue and take the glass elevator to the 9th floor.) On the way down be sure to look at the Congress Bells, cast at the same British foundry that made the bells in London's Westminster Abbey. The bells are rung to honor the opening and closing of Congress and on other important occasions, such as when the Redskins win the Super Bowl.

Cross 10th Street from the Old Post Office Pavilion. Look to your left at the delightful trompe l'oeil mural on the side of the **Lincoln Building** two blocks up. It appears as if there's a hole in the building. There's also a portrait of the building's namesake. *12th St. and Pennsylvania Ave. NW, Downtown, tel. 202/606–8691 tower; 202/289–4224 pavilion. Free. Tower early May–early Sept., weekdays 9–7:45, Sat. 10–7:45, Sun. 10–6; early Sept.–early May, weekdays 9–5, weekends 9–6. Metro: Federal Triangle.*

PENNSYLVANIA AVENUE. The capital's most historically important thoroughfare repeatedly threads through sightseeing walks. Newly inaugurated presidents travel west on Pennsylvania Avenue en route to the White House. Thomas Jefferson started the parade tradition in 1805 after taking the oath of office for his second term. He was accompanied by a few friends and a handful of congressmen. Four years later James Madison made things official by instituting a proper inaugural celebration. The flag holders on the lampposts are clues that Pennsylvania Avenue remains the city's foremost parade route. With the Capitol at one end and the White House at the other, the avenue symbolizes both the separation and the ties between these two branches of government.

When Pennsylvania Avenue first opened in 1796, it was an ugly and dangerous bog. Attempts by Jefferson to beautify the road by planting poplar trees were only partially successful: many were chopped down by fellow citizens for firewood. In the mid-19th century, crossing the rutted thoroughfare was treacherous, and rainstorms often turned the street into a river. The avenue was finally paved with wooden blocks in 1871.

At the convergence of 7th Street and Pennsylvania and Indiana avenues is a multitude of statues and monuments. The **Grand Army of the Republic** memorial pays tribute to the soldiers who won the Civil War. Less conventional is the nearby stork-surmounted **Temperance Fountain.** It was erected in the 19th century by a teetotaling physician named Cogswell who hoped the fountain, which once dispensed ice-cold water, would help lure people from the evils of drink.

Redevelopment has rejuvenated Pennsylvania Avenue and the neighboring **Pennsylvania Quarter,** the name given to the mix of condominiums, apartments, retail spaces, and restaurants in the blocks bounded by Pennsylvania Avenue and 6th, 9th, and G streets. The area includes the Lansburgh complex, at the corner of 8th and E streets. Built around three existing buildings (including the defunct Lansburgh department store), the complex includes the Shakespeare Theatre, a 447-seat space. *Metro: Archives/Navy Memorial.*

9 PETERSEN HOUSE. Lincoln died in the house of William Petersen, a tailor, on the morning of April 15, 1865, after being shot at Ford's Theatre the night before. You can see the restored front and back parlors of the house, as well as the bedroom where the president died. Call in advance for tour times. *516 10th St. NW, Downtown, tel. 202/426–6830, www.nps/gov/foth. Free. Daily 9–5. Metro: Metro Center or Gallery Place/Chinatown.*

SMITHSONIAN AMERICAN ART MUSEUM. This museum (formerly the National Museum of American Art) is housed in the Old Patent Office Building, which is under major renovation through 2005. The museum and the National Portrait Gallery, which share the building, are closed during the renovation, but the Smithsonian American Art Museum continues its public presence through its Web site and a full program at the Renwick Gallery. *8th and G Sts. NW, Downtown, tel. 202/357–2700; 202/357–1729 TDD, www.americanart.si.edu. Metro: Gallery Place/Chinatown.*

WILLARD INTER-CONTINENTAL. There was a Willard Hotel on this spot long before this ornate structure was built in 1901. The original Willard was the place to stay in Washington if you were rich or influential (or wanted to give that impression). Abraham

Lincoln stayed there while waiting to move into the nearby White House. Julia Ward Howe stayed there during the Civil War and wrote "The Battle Hymn of the Republic" after gazing down from her window to see Union troops drilling on Pennsylvania Avenue. It's said the term "lobbyist" was coined to describe the favor seekers who would buttonhole President Ulysses S. Grant in the hotel's public rooms. The second Willard, its mansard roof dotted with circular windows, was designed by Henry Hardenbergh, architect of New York's Plaza hotel. Although it was just as opulent as the hotel it replaced, it fell on hard times after World War II. In 1968 it closed, standing empty until 1986, when it reopened, amid much fanfare, after an ambitious restoration. The Willard's rebirth is one of the most visible successes of the Pennsylvania Avenue Development Corporation, the organization charged with reversing the decay of America's Main Street. *1401 Pennsylvania Ave. NW, Downtown, tel. 202/628–9100 or 800/327–0200, www. washington.interconti.com.*

GEORGETOWN

Long before the District of Columbia was formed, Georgetown, Washington's oldest and wealthiest neighborhood, was a separate city with a harbor full of ships and warehouses filled with tobacco. Washington has filled in around Georgetown over the years, but the former tobacco port retains an air of aloofness. Its narrow streets, which don't conform to Pierre-Charles L'Enfant's plan for the Federal City, host active pedestrian traffic and an active nightlife.

The area that would come to be known as George (after George II), then George Towne and, finally, Georgetown, was part of Maryland when it was settled in the early 1700s by Scottish immigrants, many of whom were attracted to the region's tolerant religious climate. Georgetown's position at the farthest point up the Potomac accessible by boat made it an ideal transit and inspection point for farmers who grew tobacco in Maryland's interior. In 1789 the state granted the town a charter, but two years later Georgetown—along with Alexandria, its counterpart in Virginia—was included by George Washington in the Territory of Columbia, site of the new capital.

While Washington struggled, Georgetown thrived. Wealthy traders built their mansions on the hills overlooking the river; merchants and the working class lived in modest homes closer to the water's edge. In 1810 a third of Georgetown's population was black—both free people and slaves. The Mt. Zion United Methodist Church on 29th Street is the oldest organized black congregation in the city. When the church stood at 27th and P streets, it was a stop on the Underground Railroad (the original building burned down in the mid-1800s). Georgetown's rich history and success instilled in all its citizens a feeling of pride that still lingers today. (When Georgetowners thought the dismal capital was dragging them down, they asked to be given back to Maryland, the way Alexandria was given back to Virginia in 1845.) Tobacco eventually became a less important commodity, and Georgetown became a milling center, using water power from the Potomac. When the Chesapeake & Ohio (C&O) Canal was completed in 1850, the city intensified its milling operations and became the eastern end of a waterway that stretched 184 mi to the west. The canal took up some of the slack when Georgetown's harbor began to fill with silt and the port lost business to Alexandria and Baltimore, but the canal never became the success it was meant to be.

In the years that followed, Georgetown was a far cry from the fashionable spot it is today. Clustered near the water were a foundry, a fish market, paper and cotton mills, and a power station for the city's streetcar system, all of which made Georgetown a smelly industrial district. It still had its Georgian, federal, and Victorian homes, though, and when the New Deal and World War II brought a flood of newcomers to Washington, Georgetown's tree-shaded streets and handsome brick houses were rediscovered. Pushed out in the process were many of Georgetown's renters, which included many of its black residents.

Today some of Washington's most famous citizens call Georgetown home, including former *Washington Post* editor Ben Bradlee, Senator Joe Lieberman, and celebrity biographer Kitty Kelley. Georgetown's historic preservationists are among the most vocal in the city. Part of what the activists want protection from is the crush of people who descend on their community every night. This is one of Washington's main areas for restaurants, bars, nightclubs, and trendy boutiques. On M Street and Wisconsin Avenue, you can indulge just about any taste and take home almost any upscale souvenir. Harder to find is a parking place.

Georgetown owes some of its charm and separate growth to geography. This town-unto-itself is separated from Washington to the east by Rock Creek. On the south it's bordered by the Potomac, on the west by Georgetown University. How far north does Georgetown reach? Probably not much farther than the large estates and parks above R Street, though developers and real estate agents would be happy to include in Georgetown all the land up to the Canadian border if it increased the value of property along the way.

There's no Metro stop in Georgetown, so you have to travel by bus, taxi, or foot to this part of Washington. It's about a 15-minute walk from the Dupont Circle or Foggy Bottom Metro station. (The G2 Georgetown University bus goes from Dupont Circle west along P Street. The 34 and 36 Friendship Heights buses leave from 22nd and Pennsylvania and deposit you at 31st and M.)

Sights to See

C&O CANAL. This waterway kept Georgetown open to shipping after its harbor had filled with silt. George Washington was one of the first to advance the idea of a canal linking the Potomac with the Ohio River across the Appalachians. Work started on the C&O Canal in 1828, and when it opened in 1850, its 74 locks linked

Georgetown with Cumberland, Maryland, 184 mi to the northwest (still short of its intended destination). Lumber, coal, iron, wheat, and flour moved up and down the canal, but it was never as successful as its planners had hoped it would be. Many of the bridges spanning the canal in Georgetown were too low to allow anything other than fully loaded barges to pass underneath, and competition from the Baltimore & Ohio Railroad eventually spelled an end to profitability. Today the canal is a part of the National Park System, and walkers follow the towpath once used by mules while canoeists paddle the canal's calm waters. Between April and November you can go on a leisurely (about an hour) mule-drawn trip aboard the *Georgetown* canal boat. Tickets are available across the canal, next to the Foundry. Barge rides are also available at Great Falls, at the end of MacArthur Boulevard, in nearby Potomac, Maryland. Barge rides are given late March through mid-June and early September through early November, Wednesday to Friday at 11 and 2:30, and on weekends at 11, 1, 2:30, and 4. From mid-June through early September, barge rides are Wednesday to Friday at 11, 1, and 2:30, and on weekends at 11, 1, 2:30, and 4; the cost is $8. *Canal Visitor Center, 1057 Thomas Jefferson St. NW, Georgetown, tel. 202/653–5190.*

❼ DUMBARTON HOUSE. Its symmetry and the two curved wings on its north side make Dumbarton, built around 1800, a distinctive example of Federal architecture. The first occupant of the house, Joseph Nourse, was registrar of the U.S. Treasury. Other well-known Americans have spent time here, including Dolley Madison, who stopped here when fleeing Washington in 1814. One hundred years later, the house was saved from demolition by being moved 100 ft up the hill, when Q Street was cut through to the Dumbarton Bridge. Since 1928, it has served as the headquarters of the National Society of the Colonial Dames of America.

Eight rooms inside Dumbarton House have been restored to federal-period splendor, with period furnishings such as mahogany American Chippendale chairs, hallmark silver,

Persian rugs, and a breakfront cabinet filled with rare books. Other notable items include Martha Washington's traveling cloak, a British redcoat's red coat, and a 1789 Charles Willson Peale portrait of the children of Benjamin Stoddert, the first secretary of the navy (the portrait has a view of Georgetown harbor in the background). In order to see the house's interior, visitors must take the guided 45-minute tour. *2715 Q St. NW, Georgetown, tel. 202/337–2288. Suggested donation $3. Labor Day–July, Tues.–Sat. 10–1 (last tour at 12:15). Tours begin at 10:15, 11:15, and 12:15.*

❻ DUMBARTON OAKS. Don't confuse Dumbarton Oaks with the nearby Dumbarton House. In 1944 one of the most important events of the 20th century took place in Dumbarton Oaks, when representatives of the United States, Great Britain, China, and the Soviet Union met in the music room here to lay the groundwork for the United Nations.

Career diplomat Robert Woods Bliss and his wife, Mildred, bought the property in 1920 and set about taming the sprawling grounds and removing later 19th-century additions that had obscured the federal lines of the 1801 mansion. In 1940 the Blisses gave the estate to Harvard University, which maintains world-renowned, albeit small, collections of Byzantine and pre-Columbian art here. The Byzantine collection includes beautiful examples of both religious and secular items executed in mosaic, metal, enamel, and ivory. Pre-Columbian works—artifacts and textiles from Mexico and Central and South America by such peoples as the Aztec, Maya, and Olmec—are arranged in an enclosed glass pavilion designed by Philip Johnson. Also on view to the public are the lavishly decorated music room and selections from Mrs. Bliss's collection of rare illustrated garden books.

Dumbarton Oaks's 10 acres of formal gardens is one of the loveliest spots in Washington (enter at 31st and R streets). Planned by noted landscape architect Beatrix Farrand, the

georgetown

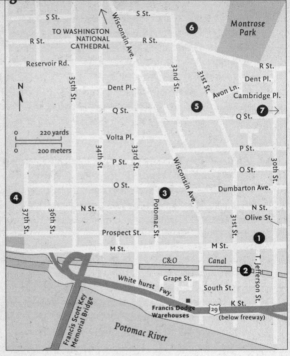

C&O Canal, 2

Dumbarton House, 7

Dumbarton Oaks, 6

Georgetown University, 4

Old Stone House, 1

St. John's Church, 3

Tudor Place, 5

gardens incorporate elements of traditional English, Italian, and French styles such as a formal rose garden, an English country garden, and an Orangery (circa 1810). A full-time crew of a dozen gardeners toils to maintain the stunning collection of terraces, geometric gardens, tree-shaded brick walks, fountains, arbors, and pools. Plenty of well-positioned benches make this a good place for resting weary feet, too. *1703 32nd St. NW, Georgetown, tel. 202/339–6401 or 202/339–6400. Art collections Tues.–Sun. 2–5. Gardens Apr.–Oct., daily 2–6; Nov.–Mar., daily 2–5.*

★ ❹ **GEORGETOWN UNIVERSITY.** Founded in 1789 by John Carroll, first American bishop and first archbishop of Baltimore, Georgetown is the oldest Jesuit school in the country. About 12,000 students attend Georgetown, known now as much for its perennially successful basketball team as for its fine programs in law, medicine, foreign service, and the liberal arts. When seen from the Potomac or from Washington's high ground, the Gothic spires of Georgetown's older buildings give the university an almost medieval look. *37th and O Sts., Georgetown, tel. 202/687–5055, www.georgetown.edu.*

❶ **OLD STONE HOUSE.** What was early American life like? Here's the capital's oldest window into the past. Work on this fieldstone house, thought to be Washington's only surviving pre-Revolutionary building, was begun in 1764 by a cabinetmaker named Christopher Layman. The house, now a museum, was used as both a residence and a place of business by a succession of occupants. Five of the house's rooms are furnished with the simple, sturdy artifacts—plain tables, spinning wheels, and so forth—of 18th-century middle-class life. The National Park Service maintains the house and its lovely gardens in the rear, which are planted with fruit trees and perennials. *3051 M St. NW, Georgetown, tel. 202/426–6851. Free. Wed.–Sun. 10–4.*

❸ **ST. JOHN'S CHURCH.** West of Wisconsin Avenue, a several-blocks-long stretch of O Street has remnants from an earlier age: cobblestones and streetcar tracks. Residents are so proud of the cobblestones that newer concrete patches have been scored to resemble them. Prominent in this section of Georgetown is one of the oldest churches in the city, St. John's Church, built in 1796 and attributed to Dr. William Thornton, architect of the Capitol. Interior alterations reflect a Victorian, rather than federal, style. St. John's is also noted for its stained-glass windows, including a small Tiffany. *3240 O St. NW, tel. 202/338–1796. Services Sun. at 9 and 11, Thurs. at 11:30.*

⑤ TUDOR PLACE. Stop at Q Street between 31st and 32nd streets; look through the trees to the north, at the top of a sloping lawn; and you'll see the neoclassical Tudor Place, designed by Capitol architect Dr. William Thornton and completed in 1816. On a house tour you'll see Francis Scott Key's desk, items that belonged to George Washington, and spurs belonging to members of the Peter family who were killed in the Civil War. The grounds contain many specimens planted in the early 19th century. The house was built for Thomas Peter, son of Georgetown's first mayor, and his wife, Martha Custis, Martha Washington's granddaughter. It was because of this connection to the president's family that Tudor Place came to house many items from Mount Vernon. The yellow stucco house is interesting for its architecture—especially the dramatic, two-story domed portico on the south side—but its familial heritage is even more remarkable: Tudor Place stayed in the same family for 178 years, until 1983, when Armistead Peter III died. Before his death, Peter established a foundation to restore the house and open it to the public. Tour reservations are advised. *1644 31st St. NW, Georgetown, tel. 202/965–0400, www.tudorplace.org. House and garden tour, suggested donation $6. House tour Tues.–Fri. at 10, 11:30, 1, and 2:30; Sat. hourly 10–4 (last tour at 3). Garden Nov.–Mar. and June–Aug., Mon.–Sat. 10–4; Apr.–May and Sept.–Oct., Mon.–Sat. 10–4, Sun. noon–4.*

WASHINGTON NATIONAL CATHEDRAL – Construction of
Washington National Cathedral—the sixth-largest cathedral
in the world—started in 1907 and finished in 1990, when the
building was consecrated. Like its 14th-century Gothic
counterparts, the stunning National Cathedral (officially the
Cathedral Church of St. Peter and St. Paul) has a nave, flying
buttresses, transepts, and vaults that were built stone by
stone. It's adorned with fanciful gargoyles created by skilled
stone carvers. The tomb of Woodrow Wilson, the only
president buried in Washington, is on the south side of the
nave. The expansive view of the city from the Pilgrim Gallery is
exceptional. The cathedral is Episcopal but has hosted services
of many denominations.

On the grounds of the cathedral is the compact, English-style
Bishop's Garden. Boxwoods, ivy, tea roses, yew trees, and an
assortment of arches, bas-reliefs, and stonework from
European ruins provide a restful counterpoint to the cathedral's
towers. *Wisconsin and Massachusetts Aves. NW, Cleveland Park, tel.
202/537–6200; 202/537–6207 tour information, www.cathedral.org.
Suggested tour donation $3. Early-May–early Sept., weekdays 10–5,
Sat. 10–4:30, Sun. 8–5; early Sept.–early May, daily 10–5. Sun.
services at 8, 9, 10, 11, and 4; evening prayer daily at 4:30; tours every
15 mins Mon.–Sat. 10–11:30 and 12:45–3:15, Sun. 12:45–2:30.*

DUPONT CIRCLE
Three of Washington's main thoroughfares intersect at Dupont
Circle: Connecticut, New Hampshire, and Massachusetts
avenues. With a small, handsome park and a splashing fountain
in the center, Dupont Circle is more than an island around which
traffic flows, making it an exception among Washington circles.
The activity spills over into the surrounding streets, one of the
liveliest, most vibrant neighborhoods in D.C.

Development near Dupont Circle started during the post–Civil War boom of the 1870s. As the city increased in stature, the nation's wealthy and influential citizens began building their mansions near the circle. The area underwent a different kind of transformation in the middle of the 20th century, when the middle and upper classes deserted Washington for the suburbs, and in the 1960s the circle became the starting point for rowdy, litter-strewn marches sponsored by countercultural groups. Today the neighborhood is once again fashionable, and its many restaurants, offbeat shops, coffeehouses, art galleries, and specialty bookstores lend it a distinctive, cosmopolitan air. Stores and clubs catering to the neighborhood's large gay community are abundant.

Sights to See

❸ **ANDERSON HOUSE.** A palatial home that's a mystery even to many longtime Washingtonians, Anderson House isn't an embassy, though it does have a link to that world. Larz Anderson was a diplomat whose career included postings to Japan and Belgium. Anderson and his heiress wife, Isabel, toured the world, picking up objects that struck their fancy. They filled their residence, which was constructed in 1905, with the booty of their travels, including choir stalls from an Italian Renaissance church, Flemish tapestries, and a large—if spotty—collection of Asian art. All this remains in the house for you to see.

In accordance with the Andersons' wishes, the building also serves as the headquarters of a group to which Larz belonged: the Society of the Cincinnati. The oldest patriotic organization in the country, the society was formed in 1783 by a group of officers who had served with George Washington during the Revolutionary War. The group took its name from Cincinnatus, a distinguished Roman farmer who, circa 500 BC, led an army against Rome's enemies and later quelled civil disturbances in the city. After each success, rather than seek political power that could have easily been his, he returned to the simple life on his farm. The story impressed the American officers, who saw in it a mirror of their own situation: they, too, would leave the battlefields to get on with the business of forging a new nation. (One such member went on to name the city in Ohio.) Today's members are direct descendants of those American revolutionaries.

Many of the displays in the society's museum focus on the colonial period and the Revolutionary War. One room—painted in a marvelous trompe l'oeil style that makes the walls seem as if they're covered with sculpture—is filled with military miniatures from the United States and France. The house is often used by the federal government to entertain visiting dignitaries. Amid the glitz, glamour, beauty, and patriotic spectacle of the mansion are two painted panels in the solarium that depict the Andersons' favorite motorcar sightseeing routes around Washington. *2118 Massachusetts Ave. NW, Dupont Circle, tel. 202/785–2040. Free. Tues.–Sat. 1–4. Metro: Dupont Circle.*

4 BISON BRIDGE. Tour guides at the Smithsonian's National Museum of Natural History are quick to remind you that America never had buffalo; the big, shaggy animals that roamed the plains were bison. (True buffalo are African and Asian animals of the same family.) Officially called the Dumbarton Bridge—though locals call it the Bison Bridge, thanks to the four bronze statues designed by A. Phimister Proctor—the structure stretches across Rock Creek Park into Georgetown. Its sides are decorated with busts of Native Americans, the work of architect Glenn Brown, who, along with his son Bedford, designed the bridge in 1914. The best way to see the busts is to walk the footpath along Rock Creek. *23rd and Q Sts. NW, Dupont Circle and Georgetown. Metro: Dupont Circle.*

1 DUPONT CIRCLE. Originally known as Pacific Circle, this hub was the westernmost circle in Pierre-Charles L'Enfant's original design for the Federal City. The name was changed in 1884, when

dupont circle and foggy bottom

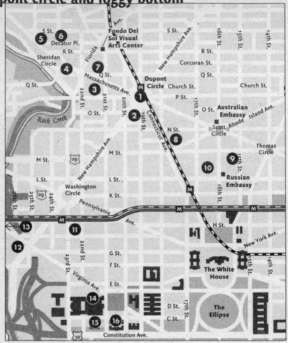

Congress authorized construction of a bronze statue honoring Civil War hero Admiral Samuel F. Dupont. The statue fell into disrepair, and Dupont's family—who had never liked it anyway—replaced it in 1921. The marble fountain that stands in its place, with allegorical figures Sea, Stars, and Wind, was created by Daniel Chester French, the sculptor of Lincoln's statue in the Lincoln Memorial.

As you look around the circumference of the circle, you can see the special constraints within which architects in Washington must work. Since a half dozen streets converge on Dupont Circle, the buildings around it are, for the most part, wedge-shaped and set on plots of land formed like massive slices of pie. Only two of the great houses that stood on the circle in the early 20th century remain today. The Renaissance-style house at **15 Dupont Circle,** next to P Street, was built in 1903 for Robert W. Patterson, publisher of the *Washington Times-Herald.* Patterson's daughter, Cissy, who succeeded him as publisher, was known for hosting parties that attracted such notables as William Randolph Hearst, Douglas MacArthur, and J. Edgar Hoover. In 1927, while Cissy was living in New York City and the White House was being refurbished, Calvin Coolidge and his family stayed here. While they did, they received American aviator Charles Lindbergh; some of the most famous photographs of Lindy were taken as he stood on the house's balcony and smiled down at the crowds below. In 1948 Cissy willed the house to the American Red Cross, and the Washington Club, a private club, bought it from the organization in 1951. The **Sulgrave Club,** at the corner of Massachusetts Avenue, with its rounded apex facing the circle, was also once a private home and is now likewise a private club. *Metro: Dupont Circle.*

❷ HEURICH HOUSE MUSEUM. Currently housing the **Historical Society of Washington, D.C.,** this opulent Romanesque Revival was the home of Christian Heurich, a German orphan who made his fortune in the beer business. Heurich's brewery was in Foggy

Bottom, where the Kennedy Center stands today. Brewing was a dangerous business in the 19th century, and fires more than once reduced Heurich's brewery to ashes. Perhaps because of this he insisted that his home, completed in 1894, be fireproof; in fact, it was the first building in Washington with residential fireproofing. Although 17 fireplaces were installed—some with onyx facings, one with the bronze image of a lion staring out from the back—not a single one ever held a fire.

After Heurich's widow died in 1955, the house was turned over to the historical society and today houses a research library and museum. Most of the furnishings in the house were owned and used by the Heurichs. The Victorian interior is an eclectic gathering of plaster detailing, carved wooden doors, and painted ceilings. The downstairs breakfast room, in which Heurich, his wife, and their three children ate most of their meals, is decorated like a rathskeller and is adorned with such German sayings as "A good drink makes old people young."

Heurich must have taken the proverbs seriously. He drank his beer every day, had three wives (in succession), and lived to be 102. (In 1986 Heurich's grandson Gary started brewing the family beer again. Though it's made in Utica, New York, he vows to build someday another Heurich brewery near Washington.) Tours are self-guided, or you can make an advance request for a guided tour. The docents who give the tours are also adept at answering questions about other Washington landmarks. As of this writing, the Historical Society has put the Heurich House up for sale in preparation for a 2003 move into the new City Museum in the Old Downtown area. *1307 New Hampshire Ave. NW, Dupont Circle, tel. 202/785–2068, www.hswdc.org. $3. Mon.–Sat. 10–4. Metro: Dupont Circle.*

⑨ METROPOLITAN AFRICAN METHODIST EPISCOPAL CHURCH. Completed in 1886, the Gothic-style Metropolitan African Methodist Episcopal Church has become one of the most influential African-American churches in the city. Abolitionist orator Frederick Douglass worshiped here, and Bill Clinton chose the church for both of his inaugural prayer services. *1518 M St. NW, Downtown, tel. 202/331–1426. Metro: Farragut North.*

🖐 ⑩ **NATIONAL GEOGRAPHIC SOCIETY.** Founded in 1888, the society is best known for its yellow-border magazine. The society has sponsored numerous expeditions throughout its 100-year history, including those of admirals Peary and Byrd and underwater explorer Jacques Cousteau. Explorers Hall, entered from 17th Street, is the magazine come to life. It invites you to learn about the world in a decidedly interactive way: you can experience everything from a mini tornado to video touch screens that explain geographic concepts and then quiz you on what you've learned. The most dramatic events take place in Earth Station One Interactive Theatre, a 72-seat amphitheater that sends the audience on a journey around the world. The centerpiece is a hand-painted globe, 11 ft in diameter, that floats and spins on a cushion of air, showing off different features of the planet. *17th and M Sts. NW, Dupont Circle, tel. 202/857–7588; 202/857–7689 group tours. Free. Mon.–Sat. 9–5, Sun. 10–5. Metro: Farragut North.*

★ ⑦ **PHILLIPS COLLECTION.** The first permanent museum of modern art in the country, the masterpiece-filled Phillips Collection is unique both in origin and content. In 1918 Duncan Phillips, grandson of a founder of the Jones and Laughlin Steel Company, started to collect art for a museum that would stand as a memorial to his father and brother, who had died within 13 months of each other. Three years later what was first called the Phillips Memorial Art Gallery opened in two rooms of this Georgian Revival home near Dupont Circle.

Not interested in a painting's market value or its faddishness, Phillips searched for works that impressed him as outstanding products of a particular artist's unique vision. Holdings include works by Georges Braque, Paul Cézanne, Paul Klee, Henri

Matisse, John Henry Twachtman, and the largest museum collection in the country of the work of Pierre Bonnard. The exhibits change regularly. The collection's best-known paintings include Renoir's *Luncheon of the Boating Party*, *Repentant Peter* by both Goya and El Greco, *A Bowl of Plums* by 18th-century artist Jean-Baptiste Siméon Chardin, Degas's *Dancers at the Bar*, and Vincent van Gogh's *Entrance to the Public Garden at Arles*. A self-portrait of Cézanne was the painting Phillips said he would save first if the gallery caught fire. During the 1920s, Phillips and his wife, Marjorie, started to support American Modernists such as John Marin, Georgia O'Keeffe, and Arthur Dove.

The Phillips is a comfortable museum. Works of an artist are often grouped together in "exhibition units," and, unlike most other galleries (where uniformed guards appear uninterested in the masterpieces around them), the Phillips employs students of art, many of whom are artists themselves, to sit by the paintings and answer questions.

On Thursday the museum stays open late for live jazz, gallery talks, and a cash bar. From September to May, the museum hosts a Sunday afternoon concert series at 5 in the music room. It's free with museum admission. *1600 21st St. NW, Dupont Circle, tel. 202/ 387–2151, www.phillipscollection.org. $7.50. Sept.–May, Tues., Wed., Fri., and Sat. 10–5, Thurs. 10–8:30, Sun. noon–7; June–Aug., Tues., Wed., Fri., and Sat. 10–5, Thurs. 10–8:30, Sun. noon–5. Tour Wed. and Sat. at 2. Gallery talk 1st and 3rd Thurs. at 12:30. Metro: Dupont Circle.*

❽ ST. MATTHEW'S CATHEDRAL. John F. Kennedy frequently worshiped in this Renaissance-style church, the seat of Washington's Roman Catholic diocese, and in 1963 Kennedy's funeral mass was held within its richly decorated walls. Set in the floor, directly in front of the main altar, is a memorial to the slain president: "Here rested the remains of President Kennedy at the requiem mass November 25, 1963, before their removal to Arlington where they lie in expectation of a heavenly resurrection."

A memorial to nuns who served as nurses during the Civil War is across Rhode Island Avenue. *1725 Rhode Island Ave. NW, Dupont Circle, tel. 202/347–3215. Free. Weekdays and Sun. 7–6:30, Sat. 8–6:30; tour usually Sun. at 2:30. Metro: Farragut North.*

⑥ TEXTILE MUSEUM. In the 1890s, George Hewitt Myers, heir to the Bristol-Myers fortune, purchased his first Oriental rug for his dorm room at Yale. Later, Myers lived two houses down from Woodrow Wilson, at 2310 S Street, in a home designed by John Russell Pope, architect of the National Archives and the Jefferson Memorial. Myers bought the Waddy B. Wood–designed house next door, at No. 2320, and opened his museum to the public in 1925. Today the collection includes more than 17,000 textiles and carpets. Rotating exhibits are taken from a permanent collection of historic and ethnographic items that include Coptic and pre-Columbian textiles, Kashmir embroidery, and Turkman tribal rugs. At least one show of modern textiles—such as quilts or fiber art—is mounted each year. The Activity Gallery in the Textile Learning Center has hands-on exhibits and activities. You can look at several textile techniques, then try your hand at doing them yourself. *2320 S St. NW, tel. 202/667–0441, www.textilemuseum.org. Suggested donation $5. Mon.–Sat. 10–5, Sun. 1–5; highlight tour Sept.– May, Wed. and weekends at 1:30. Metro: Dupont Circle.*

⑤ WOODROW WILSON HOUSE. Until the Clintons bought a house here, Wilson was the only president who stayed in D.C. after leaving the White House. (He's also the only president buried in the city, inside the National Cathedral.) He and his second wife, Edith Bolling Wilson, retired in 1920 to this Georgian Revival designed by Washington architect Waddy B. Wood. (Wood also designed the Department of the Interior and the National Museum of Women in the Arts.) The house was built in 1915 for a carpet magnate.

President Wilson suffered a stroke toward the end of his second term, in 1919, and he lived out the last few years of his life on this quiet street. Edith made sure he was comfortable; she had a bed constructed that was the same dimension as the large Lincoln bed Wilson had slept in while in the White House. She also had the house's trunk lift (a sort of dumbwaiter for trunks) converted to an Otis elevator so the partially paralyzed president could move from floor to floor. When the streetcars stopped running in 1962 the elevator stopped working; it had received its electricity directly from the streetcar line.

Wilson died in 1924. Edith survived him by 37 years. After she died in 1961, the house and its contents were bequeathed to the National Trust for Historic Preservation. On view inside are such items as a Gobelins tapestry, a baseball signed by King George V, and the shell casing from the first shot fired by U.S. forces in World War I. The house also contains memorabilia related to the history of the short-lived but influential League of Nations, including the colorful flag Wilson hoped would be adopted by that organization. 2340 S St. NW, Dupont Circle, tel. 202/387–4062. $5. Tues.–Sun. 10–4. Metro: Dupont Circle.

FOGGY BOTTOM

The Foggy Bottom area of Washington—bordered roughly by the Potomac and Rock Creek to the west, 20th Street to the east, Pennsylvania Avenue to the north, and Constitution Avenue to the south—has three main claims to fame: the State Department, the Kennedy Center, and George Washington University. In 1763 a German immigrant named Jacob Funk purchased this land, and a community called Funkstown sprang up on the Potomac. This nickname is only slightly less amusing than the present one, an appellation derived from the wharves, breweries, lime kilns, and glassworks that were near the water. Smoke from these factories combined with the swampy air of the low-lying ground to produce a permanent fog along the waterfront.

The smoke-belching factories ensured work for the hundreds of German and Irish immigrants who settled in Foggy Bottom in the 19th century. By the 1930s, however, industry was on the way out, and Foggy Bottom had become a poor part of Washington. The opening of the State Department headquarters in 1947 reawakened middle-class interest in the neighborhood's modest row houses. Many of them are now gone, and Foggy Bottom today suffers from a split personality as tiny, one-room-wide row houses sit next to large, mixed-use developments.

Although the Foggy Bottom neighborhood has its own Metro stop, many attractions are a considerable distance away. If you don't relish long walks or time is limited, check the Foggy Bottom map to see if you need to make alternate travel arrangements to visit specific sights.

Sights to See

⑭ DEPARTMENT OF STATE. The foreign policy of the United States is formulated and administered by battalions of brainy analysts in the huge Department of State Building (often referred to as the State Department), which also serves as the headquarters of the United States Diplomatic Corps. All is presided over by the secretary of state, who is fourth in line for the presidency (after the vice president, speaker of the House, and president *pro tempore* of the Senate) should the president be unable to serve. On the top floor are the opulent Diplomatic Reception Rooms, decorated like the great halls of Europe and the rooms of colonial American plantations. The furnishings include a Philadelphia highboy, a Paul Revere bowl, and the desk on which the Treaty of Paris, which ended the Revolutionary War, was signed in 1783. The largest room has a specially loomed carpet so heavy and large it had to be airlifted in by helicopter. The rooms are used 15–20 times a week to entertain foreign diplomats and heads of state; you can see them, too, but you need to register for a tour three months in advance. The tours are recommended for those 13 and over. *2201 C St. NW, Foggy Bottom, tel. 202/647–3241; 202/736–4474 TDD, www.state.gov. Free. Tours weekdays at 9:30, 10:30, and 2:45. Metro: Foggy Bottom.*

16 **FEDERAL RESERVE BUILDING.** Whether interest rates are raised or lowered in attempts to control the economy is decided in this imposing marble edifice, its bronze entryway topped by a massive eagle. Designed by Folger Library architect Paul Cret, "the Fed" is on Constitution Avenue between 20th and 21st streets. It seems to say, "Your money's safe with us." Even so, there isn't any money here. Ft. Knox holds most of the government's gold. The Fed's stately facade belies a friendlier interior, with a varied collection of art and four special art exhibitions every year. A 45-minute tour includes a film that explains exactly what it is that the Fed does. *Enter on C St. between 20th and 21st Sts., Foggy Bottom, tel. 202/452–3000; 202/452–3149 building tours; 202/452–3686 art tours. Free. Weekdays 11–4 during art exhibitions (tours of permanent art collection by appointment only); building tour Thurs. at 2:30. Metro: Foggy Bottom.*

11 **GEORGE WASHINGTON UNIVERSITY.** George Washington had always hoped the capital would hold a world-class university. He even left 50 shares of stock in the Patowmack Canal Co. to endow it. Congress never acted upon his wishes, however, and it wasn't until 1822 that the university that would eventually be named after the first president began to take shape. The private Columbian College in the District of Columbia opened that year with the aim of training students for the Baptist ministry. In 1904 the university shed its Baptist connections and changed its name to George Washington University. In 1912 it moved to its present location and since that time has become the second largest landholder in the District (after the federal government). Students have ranged from J. Edgar Hoover to Jacqueline Bouvier. In addition to residing in modern university buildings, GWU occupies many 19th-century houses. *Downtown campus covers much of Foggy*

Bottom south of Pennsylvania Ave. between 19th and 24th Sts., Foggy Bottom, tel. 202/994–1000, www.gwu.edu. Metro: Foggy Bottom.

⑬ JOHN F. KENNEDY CENTER FOR THE PERFORMING ARTS.
Thanks to the Kennedy Center, Washington regularly hosts world-class performers. Prior to 1971, Washington after dark was primarily known for cocktail parties, not culture. The opening of the Kennedy Center in that year instantly established the capital as a locale for culture on an international scale. Concerts, ballets, opera, musicals, and drama are presented in the center's five theaters, and movies are screened periodically in the American Film Institute's theater.

The idea for a national cultural center had been proposed by President Eisenhower in 1955. John F. Kennedy had also strongly supported the idea, and after his assassination it was decided to dedicate the center to him. Some critics have called the center's square design unimaginative—it has been dubbed the cake box that the more decorative Watergate came in—but no one can deny that the building's big. The Grand Foyer, lighted by 18 1-ton Orrefors crystal chandeliers, is 630 ft long. (Even at this size it's mobbed at intermission.) Many of the center's furnishings were donated by foreign countries: the chandeliers came from Sweden; the tapestries on the walls came from Brazil, France, and Mexico; and the 3,700 tons of white Carrara marble for the interior and exterior of the building were a gift from Italy. Flags fly in the Hall of Nations and the Hall of States, and in the center of the foyer is a 7-ft-high, bronze, oddly textured bust of Kennedy by sculptor Robert Berks.

In addition to the regular performances in the five theaters, each year the Kennedy Center also produces festivals that highlight different musical traditions and cultures. The hugely popular annual open house is a free, daylong extravaganza of theater, dance, and music, with nonstop entertainment both indoors and outdoors. There also are free performances every evening at 6 on the Millennium Stage.

Two restaurants on the Roof Terrace Level range from casual fare to more formal dining. It can get noisy as jets fly overhead to nearby Ronald Reagan National Airport, but you can get one of the city's better views from the terrace: to the north are Georgetown and the National Cathedral; to the west, Theodore Roosevelt Island and Rosslyn, Virginia; and to the south, the Lincoln and Jefferson memorials. *New Hampshire Ave. and Rock Creek Pkwy. NW, tel. 202/467–4600, www.kennedy-center.org. Free. Daily 10–until end of last show. Metro: Foggy Bottom (free shuttle-bus service every 15 min to and from Kennedy Center on performance days).*

⑮ NATIONAL ACADEMY OF SCIENCES. Inscribed in Greek under the cornice is a quotation from Aristotle on the value of science—appropriate for a building that houses the offices of the National Academy of Sciences, the National Academy of Engineering, the Institute of Medicine, and the National Research Council. There are often free art exhibits here—not all of them relating to science—and, from September to May, free Sunday afternoon concerts. In front of the academy is Robert Berks's sculpture of Albert Einstein, done in the same mashed-potato style as the artist's bust of JFK in the Kennedy Center. *2100 C St. NW, Foggy Bottom, tel. 202/334–2436, www.nationalacademies.org/nas/arts. Free. Weekdays 9–5. Metro: Foggy Bottom.*

⑫ WATERGATE. Thanks to the events that took place on the night of June 17, 1972, the Watergate is possibly the world's most notorious apartment-office complex. As President Richard Nixon's aides E. Howard Hunt Jr. and G. Gordon Liddy sat in the Howard Johnson Motor Lodge across the street, five of their men were caught trying to bug the Democratic National Committee, headquartered on the building's sixth floor, in an attempt to subvert the democratic process on behalf of the then-president of the United States. A marketing company occupies the space today.

The suffix "-gate" is attached to any political scandal nowadays, but the Watergate itself was named after a monumental flight of steps that led down to the Potomac behind the Lincoln Memorial. The original Watergate was the site of band concerts until plane noise from nearby Ronald Reagan National Airport made the locale impractical.

Even before the break-in, the Watergate—which opened in 1965—was well known in the capital. Within its curving lines and behind its "toothpick" balusters have lived some of Washington's most famous—and infamous—citizens, including attorney general John Mitchell and presidential secretary Rose Mary Woods of Nixon White House fame as well as such D.C. insiders as Jacob Javits, Alan Cranston, Bob and Elizabeth Dole, and, more recently, Monica Lewinsky. The embassies of Brunei and Yemen are also in the Watergate. *2600 Virginia Ave., Foggy Bottom. Metro: Foggy Bottom.*

ADAMS-MORGAN, CLEVELAND PARK, AND THE NATIONAL ZOO

Adams-Morgan (roughly, the blocks north of Florida Avenue, between Connecticut Avenue and 16th Street NW) is Washington's most ethnically diverse neighborhood. And as is often the case, that means it's one of Washington's most interesting areas—a United Nations of cuisines, offbeat shops, and funky bars and clubs. The name itself, fashioned in the 1950s by neighborhood civic groups, serves as a symbol of the area's melting pot character: it's a conjunction of the names of two local schools, the predominantly white Adams School and the largely black Morgan School. Today Adams-Morgan also has every shade in between, with large Latin American and West African populations.

The neighborhood's grand 19th-century apartment buildings and row houses, along with its fun character, have attracted young professionals, the businesses that cater to them, the attendant parking and crowd problems, and the rise in real estate values. All this has caused some longtime Adams-Morganites to wonder if their neighborhood is in danger of becoming another Georgetown.

There's no Adams-Morgan Metro stop. It's a pleasant 15-minute walk from the Woodley Park/Zoo Metro station: walk south on Connecticut, then turn left on Calvert Street, and cross over Rock Creek Park on the Duke Ellington Bridge. Or you can get off at the Dupont Circle Metro stop and walk east to (and turn left onto) 18th Street. The heart of Adams-Morgan is at the crossroads of Adams Mill Road, Columbia Road, and 18th Street.

Cleveland Park, a tree-shaded neighborhood in northwest Washington, owes its name to onetime summer resident Grover Cleveland and its development to the streetcar line that was laid along Connecticut Avenue in the 1890s. President Cleveland and his wife, Frances Folson, escaped the heat of downtown Washington in 1886 by establishing a summer White House on Newark Street between 35th and 36th streets. Many prominent Washingtonians followed suit. When the streetcar came through in 1892, construction in the area snowballed. Developer John Sherman hired local architects to design houses and provided amenities such as a fire station and a streetcar-waiting lodge to entice home buyers out of the city and into "rural" Cleveland Park. Today the neighborhood's attractive houses and suburban character are popular with Washington professionals. (The Clevelands' retreat no longer stands, but on the same block is Rosedale, an 18th-century estate that was the home of another famous summer visitor, young Cuban refugee Elian Gonzalez, in 2000.)

Sights to See
....

1 **DISTRICT OF COLUMBIA ARTS CENTER.** A combination art gallery and performance space, the DCAC exhibits the work of local artists and is the host of offbeat plays and performance art. *2438 18th St. NW, Adams-Morgan, tel. 202/462–7833. Gallery free, performance costs vary. Wed.–Sun. 2–7, Fri.–Sat. 2–10, and during performances (generally Thurs.–Sun. 7–midnight).*

2 **MERIDIAN HOUSE AND THE WHITE-MEYER HOUSE.** These two handsome mansions were designed by John Russell Pope. The 30-room Meridian House was built in 1920 by Irwin Boyle Laughlin, scion of a Pittsburgh steel family and former ambassador to Spain. The Louis XVI–style home is furnished with parquet floors, ornamental iron grillwork, handsome moldings, period furniture, tapestries, and a garden planted with European linden trees. Next door is the Georgian-style house built for Henry White (former ambassador to France) that was later the home of the Meyer family, publishers of the *Washington Post.* The first floors of both houses are open to the public and hold periodic art exhibits with an international flavor. *1630 and 1624 Crescent Pl. NW, Adams-Morgan, tel. 202/667–6800. Free. Wed.–Sun. 2–5.*

3 **NATIONAL ZOOLOGICAL PARK.** Part of the Smithsonian Institution, the National Zoo is one of the foremost zoos in the world. Created by an Act of Congress in 1889, the 163-acre park was designed by landscape architect Frederick Law Olmsted, the man who designed the U.S. Capitol grounds. (Before the zoo opened in 1890, live animals used as taxidermists' models had been kept on the Mall.) Two of the zoo's most popular residents are Tian Tian and Mei Xiang, pandas from China. They receive visitors from 9 to 6 May through mid-September and 9 to 4:30 mid-September through April; expect a wait when the zoo is busy.

Throughout the zoo, innovative compounds show many animals in naturalistic settings, including the Great Flight Cage—a

adams-morgan/cleveland park

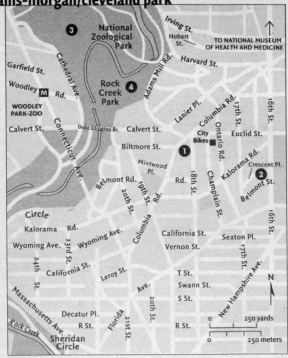

Irving St.

Hobart St.

TO NATIONAL MUSEUM
OF HEALTH AND MEDICINE

③ National
Zoological
Park

Harvard St.

Adams Mill Rd.

Garfield St.

Cathedral Ave.

Woodley
M Rd.

Rock
Creek
Park **④**

Lanier Pl.

Columbia Rd.

17th St.

16th St.

WOODLEY
PARK-ZOO

Connecticut Ave.

Duke Ellington Br.

Calvert St.

City
Bikes

Ontario Rd.

Euclid St.

Calvert St.

Calvert St.

Biltmore St.

①

Kalorama Rd.

Crescent Pl.

②

Belmont St.

Mintwood
Pl.

Rd.

18th St.

Champlain St.

Belmont Rd.

19th St.

Rd.

20th St.

Columbia
Rd.

16th St.

Circle

Kalorama   Rd.

California St.

Seaton Pl.

Wyoming Ave.

23rd St.

Wyoming Ave.

Vernon St.

17th St.

24th
St.

California St.

Leroy St.

T St.

New Hampshire Ave.

Ave.

20th St.

Swann St.

S St.

Massachusetts Ave.

Decatur Pl.

R St.

Florida

21st St.

Rock Creek

Sheridan
Circle

R St.

N

0   250 yards

0   250 meters

District of
Columbia Arts
Center, 1

Meridian House
and the
White-Meyer
House, 2

National
Zoological Park, 3

Rock Creek
Park, 4

walk-in aviary in which birds fly unrestricted from May to October (they're moved indoors during the colder months). On Lemur Island, you can see ring-tailed and red-fronted lemurs. The Cheetah Conservation Area is a grassy compound with a family of the world's fastest cats. The most ambitious addition to the zoo is Amazonia, a reproduction of a South American rain-forest ecosystem. Fish swim behind glass walls, while overhead, monkeys and birds flit from tree to tree. *3001 Connecticut Ave. NW, tel. 202/673–4800 or 202/673–4717, www.si.edu/natzoo. Free, parking $5. May–Sept. 15, daily 6 AM–8 PM; Sept. 16–Apr., daily 6–6. Zoo buildings open at 10 and close before the zoo closes. Metro: Cleveland Park or Woodley Park/Zoo.*

④ ROCK CREEK PARK. The 1,800 acres on either side of Rock Creek have provided a cool oasis for D.C. residents ever since Congress set them aside in 1890. Bicycle routes and hiking and equestrian trails wind through the groves of dogwoods, beeches, oaks, and cedar, and 30 picnic areas are scattered about. Rangers at the **Nature Center and Planetarium** (south of Military Rd., 5200 Glover Rd. NW, tel. 202/426–6829) introduce the park and keep track of daily events; guided nature walks leave from the center weekends at 2. The center and planetarium are open Wednesday through Sunday from 9 to 5. Also in the park are Ft. Reno, Ft. Bayard, Ft. Stevens, and Ft. DeRussy, remnants of the original ring of forts that guarded Washington during the Civil War, and the Rock Creek Park Golf Course, an 18-hole public course.

Landscape architect Horace Peaslee created oft-overlooked **Meridian Hill Park** (16th and Euclid Sts., Adams-Morgan), a non-contiguous section of Rock Creek Park, after a 1917 study of the parks of Europe. As a result, it contains elements of parks in France (a long, straight mall bordered with plants), Italy (terraces and wall fountains), and Switzerland (a lower-level reflecting pool based on one in Zurich). It's also unofficially known as Malcolm X Park in honor of the civil rights leader, who once spoke here. Drug activity once made it unwise to visit Meridian Hill alone: it's somewhat safer now, but avoid it after dark. *Park information, tel. 202/282–1063.*

WOODLEY PARK. Passing Cathedral Avenue (the first cross street south of the zoo), you enter a part of town known as Woodley Park. Like Cleveland Park to the north, Woodley Park grew as the streetcar advanced into this part of Washington. In 1800 Philip Barton Key, uncle of Francis Scott Key, built Woodley, a Georgian mansion on Cathedral Avenue between 29th and 31st streets. The white stucco mansion was the summer home of four presidents: Van Buren, Tyler, Buchanan, and Cleveland. It's now owned by the private Maret School. *Metro: Woodley Park/Zoo.*

ARLINGTON

There are two attractions in Arlington—both linked to the military—that should be a part of any complete visit to the nation's capital: Arlington National Cemetery and the U.S. Marine Corps War Memorial. Both are accessible by Metro, and a trip across the Potomac to Arlington is a very worthwhile half day of sightseeing.

Sights to See

★ **ARLINGTON NATIONAL CEMETERY.** More than 250,000 American war dead, as well as many notable Americans (among them presidents William Howard Taft and John F. Kennedy, General John Pershing, and Admiral Robert E. Peary), are interred in these 612 acres across the Potomac River from Washington, established as the nation's cemetery in 1864. While you're at Arlington there's a good chance you might hear the clear, doleful sound of a trumpet playing taps or the sharp reports of a gun salute. Approximately 20 funerals are held daily (it's projected that the cemetery will be filled in 2020). Although not the largest cemetery in the country, Arlington is certainly the best known, a place where you can trace America's history through the aftermath of its battles.

An important part of any visit to Arlington National Cemetery is a visit to the **Kennedy graves** (Sheridan and Weeks Drs.), where John F. Kennedy is buried under an eternal flame near two of his children, who died in infancy, and his wife, Jacqueline Bouvier Kennedy Onassis. The graves are a short walk west of the visitor center. Across from them is a low wall engraved with quotations from Kennedy's inaugural address. The public has been able to visit JFK's grave since 1967; it's now the most-visited grave site in the country. Nearby, marked by a simple white cross, is the grave of his brother Robert Kennedy.

Many distinguished veterans are buried in **Section 7A** (Crook Walk near Roosevelt Dr.) of Arlington National Cemetery near the **Tomb of the Unknowns,** including boxing champ Joe Louis, ABC newsman Frank Reynolds, actor Lee Marvin, and World War II fighter pilot Colonel "Pappy" Boyington. More than 3,800 former slaves are buried in **Section 27** (Ord and Weitzel Dr. near Custis Walk) of Arlington National Cemetery. They're all former residents of Freedman's Village, which operated at the Custis-Lee estate for more than 30 years beginning in 1863 to provide housing, education, and employment training for ex-slaves who had traveled to the capital. In the cemetery, the headstones are marked with their names and the word "Civilian" or "Citizen." Buried at Grave 19 in the first row of Section 27 is William Christman, a Union private, and the first soldier interred at Arlington National Cemetery during the Civil War.

In the United States, the first burial at the **Tomb of the Unknowns** (end of Crook Walk) took place at Arlington National Cemetery on November 11, 1921, when the Unknown Soldier World War I was interred under the large white-marble sarcophagus. Unknown servicemen killed in World War II and Korea were buried in 1958. The unknown serviceman killed in Vietnam was laid to rest on the plaza on Memorial Day 1984 but was disinterred and identified in 1998. It was decided to leave the Vietnam War unknown crypt vacant. Soldiers from the Army's U.S. 3rd Infantry ("The Old Guard") keep watch over the tomb 24 hours a day, regardless of weather conditions. The guard is changed with a precise ceremony during the day— every half hour from April through September and every hour the rest of the year. At night the guard is changed every hour.

The Memorial Amphitheater west of the tomb is the scene of special ceremonies on Veterans Day, Memorial Day, and Easter. Across from the amphitheater are memorials to the astronauts killed in the *Challenger* shuttle explosion and to the servicemen killed in 1980 while trying to rescue American hostages in Iran. Rising beyond that is the mainmast of the USS *Maine*, the American ship that was sunk in Havana Harbor in 1898, killing 299 men and sparking the Spanish-American War.

To get to Arlington National Cemetery, you can take the Metro, travel on a Tourmobile bus, or walk across Arlington Memorial Bridge (southwest of the Lincoln Memorial). If you're driving, there's a large paid parking lot at the skylighted visitor center on Memorial Drive. Stop at the center for a free brochure with a detailed map of the cemetery. If you're looking for a specific grave, the staff can consult microfilm records and give you directions to it. You should know the deceased's full name and, if possible, his or her branch of service and year of death.

Tourmobile tour buses leave from just outside the visitor center April through September, daily 8:30–6:30, and October through March, daily 8:30–4:30. You can buy tickets here for the 40-minute tour of the cemetery, which includes stops at the Kennedy grave sites, the Tomb of the Unknowns, and Arlington House. Touring the cemetery on foot means a fair bit of hiking, but it can give you a closer look at some of the thousands of graves spread over these rolling Virginia hills. If you decide to walk, head west from the visitor center on Roosevelt Drive and then turn right on Weeks Drive. *West end of Memorial Bridge, tel. 703/607–8052 to locate a grave, www.arlingtoncemetery.com. Cemetery free; parking $1.50 for the first three hours. Tourmobile $4.50. Apr.– Sept., daily 8–7; Oct.–Mar., daily 8–5.*

PENTAGON. This office building, the headquarters of the United States Department of Defense, is the largest in the world. It's twice the size of the Merchandise Mart in Chicago, and has three times the floor space of the Empire State Building in New York. The Capitol could fit into any one of its five wedge-shape sections. Approximately 23,000 military and civilian workers arrive daily. Astonishingly, this mammoth office building was completed in 1943 after fewer than two years of construction.

The structure is being reconstructed following the September 2001 crash of hijacked American Airlines Flight 77 into the northwest side of the building. At this writing, all of the areas damaged by the terrorist attack are scheduled to be renovated by spring 2003. The Pentagon Renovation Program has a Web site at www.renovation.pentagon.mil. At this writing, tours of the building are given on a very limited basis to educational groups by advance reservation, and tours for the general public have been suspended indefinitely. *I–395 at Columbia Pike and Rte. 27, tel. 703/695–1776, www.defenselink.mil/pubs/pentagon.*

UNITED STATES MARINE CORPS WAR MEMORIAL. Better known simply as "the Iwo Jima," this memorial, despite its familiarity, has lost none of its power to stir the emotions. Honoring Marines who have given their lives since the Corps was formed in 1775, the statue, sculpted by Felix W. de Weldon, is based on Joe Rosenthal's Pulitzer Prize–winning photograph of five Marines and a Navy corpsman raising a flag atop Mt. Suribachi on the Japanese island of Iwo Jima on February 19,

Smart Sightseeings

Savvy travelers and others who take their sightseeing seriously have skills worth knowing about.

DON'T PLAN YOUR VISIT IN YOUR HOTEL ROOM Don't wait until you pull into town to decide how to spend your days. It's inevitable that there will be much more to see and do than you'll have time for: choose sights in advance.

ORGANIZE YOUR TOURING Note the places that most interest you on a map, and visit places that are near each other during the same morning or afternoon.

START THE DAY WELL EQUIPPED Leave your hotel in the morning with everything you need for the day—maps, medicines, extra film, your guidebook, rain gear, and another layer of clothing in case the weather turns cooler.

TOUR MUSEUMS EARLY If you're there when the doors open you'll have an intimate experience of the collection.

EASY DOES IT See museums in the mornings, when you're fresh, and visit sit-down attractions later on. Take breaks before you need them.

STRIKE UP A CONVERSATION Only curmudgeons don't respond to a smile and a polite request for information. Most people appreciate your interest in their home town. And your conversations may end up being your most vivid memories.

GET LOST When you do, you never know what you'll find—but you can count on it being memorable. Use your guidebook to help you get back on track. Build wandering-around time into every day.

QUIT BEFORE YOU'RE TIRED There's no point in seeing that one extra sight if you're too exhausted to enjoy it.

TAKE YOUR MOTHER'S ADVICE Go to the bathroom when you have the chance. You never know what lies ahead.

1945. By executive order, a real flag flies 24 hours a day from the 78-ft-high memorial. On Tuesday evening at 7 from late May to late August there's a Marine Corps sunset parade on the grounds of the memorial. On parade nights a free shuttle bus runs from the Arlington Cemetery visitors' parking lot.

In This Chapter

Updated by Kristi Devlin

eating out

THE INFUSION OF CULTURES in the nation's capital means that, despite the dearth of ethnic neighborhoods and the kinds of restaurant districts found in many other cities, you *can* find almost any type of food here, from Burmese to Ethiopian. Even the city's French-trained chefs, who have traditionally set the standard in fine dining, have been turning to health-conscious contemporary cuisine, spicy southwestern recipes, or appetizer-size Spanish tapas for inspiration.

In Chinatown (centered on G and H streets NW between 6th and 8th), the city's one officially recognized ethnic enclave, Burmese, Thai, and other Asian cuisines add variety to the many traditional Chinese restaurants. The latter entice you with huge, brightly lit signs and offer such staples as beef with broccoli or *kung pao* chicken in a spicy sauce with roasted peanuts. But discriminating diners will find far better food at the smaller, less obvious restaurants. Look for recent reviews in *Washingtonian* magazine, the *Washington Post*, and the *Washington Times*; proud restaurant owners display good reviews on doors or in windows.

For fine dining, don't overlook restaurants in the city's luxury hotels. The formal dining room at the Willard Inter-Continental, Seasons at the Four Seasons, Citronelle at the Latham, and the dining room at the Morrison-Clark Inn are noteworthy. The cuisine is often artful and fresh. Of course, such attention to detail comes at a price. One less expensive way to experience these nationally recognized restaurants is a weekday lunch.

PRICES

The restaurants we list are the cream of the crop in each price category.

CATEGORY	COST*
$$$$	over $32
$$$	$22–$32
$$	$12–$22
$	under $12

*per person for a main course at dinner

HOW AND WHEN

It's always a good idea to make reservations; we mention them only when they're essential or are not accepted. However, even when reservations are not accepted, large groups should call ahead. All restaurants we list are open daily for lunch and dinner unless stated otherwise. Dress is mentioned only when men are required to wear a jacket or a jacket and tie, but gentlemen may be more comfortable wearing jackets and/or ties in $$$ and $$$$ restaurants, even when there is no formal dress code.

ADAMS-MORGAN/WOODLEY PARK

African

$ **MESKEREM.** Ethiopian restaurants abound in Adams-Morgan, but
★ Meskerem is distinctive for its bright, appealingly decorated dining room and the balcony, where you can eat Ethiopian-style, seated on the floor on leather cushions, with large woven baskets for tables. Entrées are served family-style on a large piece of *injera*, a sourdough flat bread; you scoop up mouthful-size portions of the hearty dishes with extra injera. Specialties include stews made with spicy *berbere* chili sauce; *kitfo*, buttery beef served raw like steak tartare or very rare; and a tangy, green-chili–vinaigrette potato salad. *2434 18th St. NW, Adams-Morgan, tel. 202/462–4100. Reservations essential. AE, DC, MC, V. Metro: Woodley Park/Zoo.*

Asian

$–$$ SAIGON GOURMET. Service is brisk and friendly at this popular, French-influenced Vietnamese restaurant. The upscale neighborhood patrons return for the ultracrisp *cha-gio* (spring rolls), the savory *pho* (beef broth), seafood soups, and the delicately seasoned and richly sauced entrées. Shrimp Saigon mixes prawns and pork in a peppery marinade, and another Saigon dish—grilled pork with rice crepes—is a Vietnamese variation on Chinese moo shu. *2635 Connecticut Ave. NW, Woodley Park, tel. 202/265–1360. Reservations essential. AE, D, DC, MC, V. Metro: Woodley Park/Zoo.*

Contemporary

$$–$$$ CASHION'S EAT PLACE. Walls are hung with family photos and tables are jammed with regulars feasting on up-to-date, home-style cooking in Ann Cashion's very personal restaurant. The menu changes daily, but roast chicken, steak, and seafood are frequent choices. Side dishes, such as garlicky mashed potatoes or buttery potatoes Anna, sometimes upstage the main course. If they're available, don't miss the goat cheese ice cream or the chocolate terrine prepared by pastry chef Beth Christianson: five layers of walnuts, caramel, mousse, and ganache. A big local attraction is Sunday brunch, when many entrées are a fraction of the normal price. *1819 Columbia Rd. NW, Adams-Morgan, tel. 202/ 797–1819. MC, V. Closed Mon. No lunch Tues.–Sat. Metro: Woodley Park/Zoo.*

$$ FELIX. With neon on the exterior and a stylized cityscape in the dining room, Felix may look more like a nightclub than a restaurant, but the contemporary cooking allays any fears. Start with tuna tartare with miso and a side of tomatillos and kumquats. A popular entrée is Alaskan halibut beside a bed of risotto made with Israeli couscous and fava beans. On Fridays, try an unexpected treat— challah, matzo-ball soup, and brisket. At 11 PM on Friday and Saturday, Felix eases into nightclub mode: live music is performed and the downstairs lounge has upscale bar food. *2406 18th St. NW,*

adams-morgan/woodley park dining

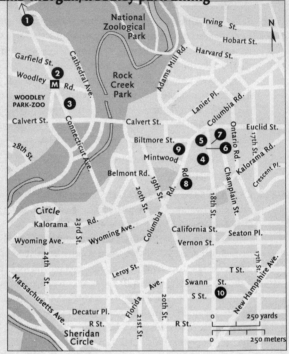

Adams-Morgan, tel. 202/483–3549. AE, DC, MC, V. No lunch. Metro: Woodley Park/Zoo.

French

$$–$$$ LA FOURCHETTE. On a block in Adams-Morgan where restaurants seem to open and close weekly, La Fourchette has stayed in business for nearly a quarter of a century by offering good-quality bistro food at reasonable prices. Most of the menu consists of daily specials, but you can pretty much count on finding bouillabaisse and rabbit on the list; other entrées might be chicken in beurre blanc or sweetbreads in a mushroom-cream sauce. La Fourchette looks as a bistro should, with an exposed-brick wall, a tin ceiling, bentwood chairs, and quasi-postimpressionist murals. Brunch is a weekend attraction with quality food at very reasonable prices. *2429 18th St. NW, Adams-Morgan, tel. 202/332–3077. AE, DC, MC, V. Metro: Woodley Park/Zoo.*

Italian

$–$$ I MATTI. Local restaurant entrepreneur and Italy native Roberto Donna owns the much more expensive Galileo, downtown, in addition to this less formal trattoria, which serves a varied menu of sophisticated dishes to a largely neighborhood clientele. Thin, crisp-crust pizzas or pasta make good lunches or light snacks. Meat and fish dishes—which might include rabbit, veal, or *bollito misto* (meat and capon cooked in a flavorful broth)—are pricier but well worth it. Service is often perfunctory, particularly on busy weekend evenings. *2436 18th St. NW, Adams-Morgan, tel. 202/462–8844. AE, DC, MC, V. No lunch Sun.–Thurs. Metro: Woodley Park/Zoo.*

Latin American

$$ GRILL FROM IPANEMA. Brazilian cuisine is the focus at the Grill, from spicy seafood stews to grilled steak and other hearty meat dishes. Appetizers include fried yucca with spicy sausages and—for adventurous eaters—fried alligator. Former Second Lady Tipper

Gore adores the *mexilhão á carioca*, garlicky mussels cooked in a clay pot. Traditional feijoada, the national dish of Brazil, is served every day. *1858 Columbia Rd. NW, Adams-Morgan, tel. 202/986–0757. AE, D, DC, MC, V. No lunch weekdays. Metro: Woodley Park/Zoo.*

$–$$ LAURIOL PLAZA. This longtime favorite on the border of Adams-Morgan and Dupont Circle serves Latin American, Cuban, and Spanish dishes—ceviche, paella, fajitas, and so on—to enthusiastic crowds. Rustic entrées such as Cuban-style pork and *lomo saltado* (Peruvian-style strip steak with onions, tomatoes, and fiery jalapeño peppers) are specialties. The dining room can get noisy, but the roof terrace of the modern, custom-design building is an airy alternative in good weather. The two hours of free parking for customers is especially enticing: this street is disputably the most difficult place to park in the city. *1835 18th St. NW, Adams-Morgan, tel. 202/387–0035. Reservations not accepted. AE, D, DC, MC, V. Metro: Dupont Circle.*

Middle Eastern

$$ LEBANESE TAVERNA. Arched ceilings, cedar panels etched with leaf patterns, woven rugs, and brass lighting fixtures give the Taverna a warm elegance. Start with an order of Arabic bread, baked in a wood-burning oven. Lamb, beef, chicken, and seafood are either grilled on kabobs, slow-roasted, or smothered with a garlicky yogurt sauce. A group can make a meal of the *mezza* platters—a mix of appetizers and sliced *shawarma* (spit-roasted lamb). *2641 Connecticut Ave. NW, Woodley Park, tel. 202/265–8681. AE, D, DC, MC, V. Metro: Woodley Park/Zoo.*

CAPITOL HILL

American

$$–$$$$ THE CAPITAL GRILLE. Just a few blocks from the U.S. Capitol on Pennsylvania Avenue, this New England steak house is a favorite among Republican Congressmen. Politics aside, the cuisine, wine list, and decor are top shelf. Don't let the aging meat in the window fool you; this upscale steak house has a lot more to offer than meat and potatoes (though there are fine dry-aged porterhouse cuts and sinful cream-based potatoes). Don't miss the pan-fried calamari with hot cherry peppers. *601 Pennsylvania Ave., Capitol Hill, tel. 202/737–6200. AE, D, DC, MC, V. No lunch weekends. Metro: Navy Memorial/Archives.*

$$–$$$ **MONOCLE.** The nearest restaurant to the Senate side of the Capitol, Monocle is a great place to spot members of Congress at lunch and dinner. The regional American cuisine is rarely adventurous but is thoroughly reliable. The crab cakes, either as a platter or a sandwich, are a specialty, and, depending on the day of the week, you might encounter pot roast or a first-rate fish dish as a special. Still, the draw here is the old-style Capitol Hill atmosphere. *107 D St. NE, Capitol Hill, tel. 202/546–4488. AE, DC, MC, V. Closed weekends. Metro: Union Station.*

French

$$–$$$$ **LA COLLINE.** Chef Robert Gréault has worked to make La Colline
★ one of the city's best French restaurants. The seasonal menu emphasizes fresh vegetables and seafood, from simple grilled preparations to fricassees and gratins with imaginative sauces. Some additional choices are duck with orange or cassis sauce and veal with chanterelle mushrooms. *400 N. Capitol St. NW, Capitol Hill, tel. 202/737–0400. AE, D, DC, MC, V. Closed Sun. No lunch Sat. Metro: Union Station.*

$–$$$ **LA BRASSERIE.** One of the Hill's most pleasant and satisfying restaurants for breakfast, lunch, or dinner, La Brasserie occupies two floors of adjoining town houses and has outdoor dining in the warmer months. The basically French menu changes seasonally, though poached salmon and breast of duck are always available. Likewise, the small, selective wine list changes often. *239 Massachusetts Ave. NE, Capitol Hill, tel. 202/546–9154. AE, D, DC, MC, V. No breakfast or lunch Sat. Metro: Union Station.*

Indian

$–$$ AATISH. Aatish means volcano, an appropriate name for a restaurant specializing in tandoori cooking—meats, seafood, vegetables, and breads cooked in the intense heat of a clay oven. What distinguishes this restaurant is the quality of its cooking: the appetizer samosa is a model version, with flaky pastry enclosing a delicious spiced mixture of potatoes and peas. The tandoori chicken is moist and delicious. Lamb dishes are very well-prepared, especially the lamb *karahi*, sautéed in a wok with ginger, garlic, tomatoes, vegetables, and spices. *609 Pennsylvania Ave. SE, Capitol Hill, tel. 202/544–0931. Reservations essential. AE, D, MC, V. Metro: Eastern Market.*

Italian

$$–$$$ BAROLO. Chef Roberto Donna of the downtown standout Galileo has his hand in some of the best Italian restaurants in town. This one is a collaboration with Enzo Fargione, Donna's cooking-school friend and a former sous-chef at Galileo. Barolo specializes in the food of their native Piedmont region. Fargione has a sure hand with pastas (fettuccine with asparagus and black-truffle sauce), fish (baked salmon on a bed of asparagus), and game (quail with truffle-shallot sauce and a red pepper timbale). *Union Station, 223 Pennsylvania Ave. SE, Capitol Hill, tel. 202/547–5011. Reservations essential. AE, D, DC, MC, V. Closed Sun. No lunch weekends. Metro: Capitol South.*

Southern

$$–$$$ B. SMITH'S. If you're in the mood for shrimp and grits, Southern-influenced B. Smith's is the spot for you. For appetizers, try the grilled cheddar cheese grits or the jambalaya—but skip the overly breaded fried green tomatoes and the too-sweet sweet potatoes. Signature entrée Swamp Thing may not sound pretty, but this mix of mustard-seasoned shrimp and crawfish with collard greens is delicious. Seafood and anything with barbecue sauce are highly recommended. *Union Station, 50 Massachusetts Ave. NE, Capitol Hill, tel. 202/289–6188. Reservations essential. AE, D, DC, MC, V. Metro: Union Station.*

DOWNTOWN

African

$$$$ **MARRAKESH.** In a part of the city better known for auto-supply
★ shops, Marrakesh provides a bit of Morocco with a fixed-price ($32, not including drinks) feast shared by everyone at your table. Appetizers consist of a platter of three salads followed by *b'stella*, a chicken version of Morocco's traditional pie made with crisp layers of phyllo dough and seasoned with cinnamon. The first main course is chicken with lemon and olive. A beef or lamb dish is next, followed by vegetable couscous, fruit, mint tea, and pastries. Flat bread, served with the meal, is used as a scoop instead of silverware. Belly dancers perform nightly. *617 New York Ave. NW, Downtown, tel. 202/393–9393. Reservations essential. No credit cards. Lunch for groups of 10 or more only, by reservation. Metro: Mt. Vernon/UDC.*

American

$$–$$$ **OLD EBBITT GRILL.** People flock here to drink at the several bars, which seem to go on for miles, and to enjoy well-prepared Buffalo chicken wings, hamburgers, and Reuben sandwiches. The Old Ebbitt also has Washington's most popular oyster bar (called "raw bar" locally), which serves farm-raised oysters from certified waters. Pasta is homemade, and daily fresh fish or steak specials are served until 1 AM. Despite the crowds, the restaurant never feels cramped, thanks to its well-spaced, comfortable booths. Service can be slow at lunch; if you're in a hurry, try the café-style Ebbitt Express next door. *675 15th St. NW, Downtown, tel. 202/347–4800. AE, D, DC, MC, V. Metro: Metro Center.*

washington dining

La Brasserie, 44
La Colline, 39
Marrakesh, 32
Monocle, 43
Nora, 12
Occidental Grill, 30
Old Ebbitt Grill, 31

Palm, 24
Pizzeria Paradiso, 15
Sala Thai, 17
1789, 5
Skewers/Café Luna, 27
Sushi-Ko, 1

Taberna del Alabardero, 20
Teaism, 9
TenPenh, 35
Tosca, 34
Two Amys, 3
Vidalia, 22

Asian

$$–$$$ TENPENH. One of the closest restaurants to the White House, this hopping venue is always buzzing with socialites, political junkies, and politicians. Chef Jeff Tunks's menu draws from many Asian cuisines—Chinese, Japanese, Thai, Vietnamese, even Filipino—but even the pickiest of eaters is likely to find something appealing here. An appetizer of spiced fried quail with green-papaya salad combines two favorite Vietnamese dishes. Main courses range from Tunks's signature Chinese smoked lobster to lamb chops with an Asian pesto crust. *10th St. and Pennsylvania Ave. NW, Downtown, tel. 202/393–4500. Reservations essential. AE, D, DC, MC, V. Closed Sun. Metro: Navy Archives.*

$$ KAZ SUSHI BISTRO. Traditional Japanese cookery is combined with often inspired improvisations ("freestyle Japanese cuisine," in the words of chef–owner Kaz Okochi) at this serene location. For a first-rate experience, sit at the sushi bar and ask for whatever is freshest and best. You might be surprised with buttery fatty tuna, fresh shrimp, or monkfish liver. It's not all sushi here: other innovations include sake-poached scallops with lemon-cilantro dressing. *1915 I St. NW, Downtown, tel. 202/530–5500. AE, DC, MC, V. Closed Sun. No lunch weekends. Metro: Farragut West.*

$ TEAISM. A stock of more than 50 teas (black, white, and green) imported from India, Japan, and Africa is the main source of pride for this tranquil tea house. But the tea doesn't outshine the healthy and delicious Japanese, Indian, and Thai food. Diners mix small dishes—tandoori kabobs, tea-cured salmon, Indian flat breads, salads, and various chutneys—to create meals or snacks. For the adventurous diner there's a juicy ostrich burger or *ochazuke*, green tea poured over seasoned rice. Japanese *bento* boxes come with a salad, entrée, rice, and cookies. *400 8th St., NW, Downtown, tel. 202/638–7740. Breakfast served; closes at 9 PM weekends. AE, MC, V. Metro: Navy/Archives. Branch: 800 Connecticut Ave., NW, Downtown, tel. 202/835–2233. Closed weekends, no dinner, breakfast served. AE, MC, V. Metro: Farragut West.*

Contemporary

$$–$$$$ **OCCIDENTAL GRILL.** One of the most venerable restaurants in the city, the popular Occidental Grill covers its walls with photos of politicians and other notables who have dined here, and the service is attentive. Tried and true dishes are best—chopped salad, grilled tuna, veal meat loaf. Over half of the menu is seafood. *Willard Inter-Continental, 1475 Pennsylvania Ave. NW, Downtown, tel. 202/783–1475. Reservations essential. AE, DC, MC, V. Metro: Metro Center.*

$$–$$$ **VIDALIA.** There's a lot more to chef Jeffrey Buben's distinguished
★ restaurant than the Vidalia onion, which is a specialty in season. Inspired by the cooking and the ingredients of the South and the Chesapeake Bay region, Buben's version of New American cuisine revolves around the best seasonal fruits, vegetables, and seafood he can find. Don't miss the roasted onion soup with spoon bread, the shrimp on yellow grits, or the sensational lemon chess pie. *1990 M St. NW, Dupont Circle, tel. 202/659–1990. AE, D, DC, MC, V. Closed Sun. July–Aug. No lunch weekends. Metro: Dupont Circle.*

$ **BREAD LINE.** Crowded, quirky, sometimes chaotic, this restaurant specializes in breads and bread-based foods and not only makes the city's best baguette but also some of its best sandwiches. Owner Mark Furstenburg makes everything on the premises, from the breakfast bagels and muffins to the ciabatta loaves for the tuna salad sandwich with preserved lemons. It's best to arrive early or late to avoid the noontime rush. Outdoor seating is available in warmer months. *1751 Pennsylvania Ave. NW, Downtown, tel. 202/822–8900. Reservations not accepted. AE, MC, V. Closed weekends. No dinner. Metro: Farragut West.*

Eclectic

$$$ **KINKEAD'S.** This multichambered restaurant has a downstairs raw bar and more-formal dining rooms upstairs. The open kitchen upstairs allows you to watch chef Robert Kinkead and company turn out an eclectic menu of mostly seafood dishes, inspired by Kinkead's New England roots and by the cooking of Asia and Latin America. Don't miss their signature dish, the pepper-crusted salmon with a ragout of crab, shrimp, corn, and chili. The menu also has a broad selection of grilled fish made simply, without sauces. The chocolate and caramel sampler, which includes a chocolate-and-caramel soufflé, is a knockout. *2000 Pennsylvania Ave. NW, Foggy Bottom, tel. 202/296–7700. Reservations essential. AE, D, DC, MC, V. Metro: Foggy Bottom/GWU.*

French

$$$–$$$$ **GERARD'S PLACE.** Don't let the simplicity of the name cause
★ you to underestimate this sophisticated spot owned by acclaimed French chef Gerard Pangaud. In the striking dining room you're served dishes with intriguing combinations of ingredients—to name a few: Gerard's signature poached lobster with a ginger, lime, and Sauternes sauce; venison served with dried fruits and pumpkin and beetroot purees; or seared tuna with black olives and roasted red peppers. If your appetite and wallet are willing, you might try the five-course fixed-price ($78) dinner. *915 15th St. NW, Downtown, tel. 202/737–4445. Reservations essential. AE, DC, MC, V. Closed Sun. No lunch Sat. Metro: McPherson Square.*

Indian

$$ **BOMBAY CLUB.** Just one block from the White House, the beautiful
★ Bombay Club tries to re-create the solace the Beltway elite might have found in a private club had they been 19th-century British colonials in India rather than modern-day Washingtonians. Potted palms and a bright blue ceiling above white plaster moldings adorn the elegant and decorous dining room. On the menu are unusual seafood specialties and a large number of vegetarian dishes, but the real standouts are the breads and the seafood appetizers. *815 Connecticut Ave. NW, Downtown, tel. 202/659–3727. Reservations essential. Jacket required. AE, DC, MC, V. No lunch Sat. Metro: Farragut West.*

Italian

$$$–$$$$ **GALILEO.** Sophisticated Piedmontese-style cooking is served at
★ the flagship restaurant of Washington entrepreneur–chef Roberto
Donna. To get the full Galileo experience, order an antipasto, a
pasta, and a main course of grilled fish, game, or veal. Four-
course ($60) and six-course ($80) fixed-price menus can be a
good value. Galileo is open for breakfast weekdays. Donna cooks
in his intimate restaurant within a restaurant, Laboratorio da
Galileo, several nights a week. Snag one of the 25 seats for an up-
close view of the master at work and a 12-course meal ($98
weekdays and $110 weekends). Reservations for the Laboratorio
must be made months in advance. 1110 21st St. NW, Downtown, tel.
202/293–7191. AE, D, DC, MC, V. No lunch weekends. Metro: Foggy
Bottom/GWU.

$$–$$$ **TOSCA.** Chef Cesare Lanfranconi spent several years in the kitchen
at Washington's best Italian restaurant, Galileo, before starting
sleek and sophisticated Tosca. The food draws heavily from
Lanfranconi's native Lake Como region of Italy, but isn't limited
by it. Combinations of American ingredients and Italian technique
are sometimes dazzling. Polenta topped with wild mushrooms is
a good example: the sweet corn taste is intense but tempered by
the mushrooms' earthiness. Pasta dishes include a delicious
ravioli stuffed with ricotta and crushed amaretto cookies. Save room
for dessert, particularly the deconstructed tiramisu. 1112 F St.
NW, Downtown, tel. 202/367–1990. AE, DC, MC, V. No lunch weekends.
Metro: Metro Center.

Latin American

$$–$$$ **CAFÉ ATLÁNTICO.** The menu is always exciting, and often
adventurous at this *nuevo Latino* restaurant with friendly service.
Guacamole made table-side by your waiter is unmistakably fresh.
If it's available, try the Pierna Ve Conejo, a rabbit leg with red beet,
rice, and fried onion or the *Vieiras con Solterito* seared scallops. The
bar makes a mean pisco sour cocktail with grape brandy. Beverages

are worth noting, with an excellent wine list comprised mostly of South American wines and California Zinfandels. Two of the best deals in town for brunch are Saturday's 20-course tasting menu for $20, and the à la carte Mexican brunch on Sunday. 405 8th St. NW, Downtown, tel. 202/393–0812. Reservations essential. AE, DC, MC, V. Metro: Archives/Navy Memorial.

Southern

$$–$$$ GEORGIA BROWN'S. An elegant "new South" eatery and a favorite hangout of local politicians, Georgia Brown's serves shrimp Carolina-style (with the head intact and steaming grits on the side); beef tenderloin medallions with a bourbon–pecan sauce; thick, rich crab soup; and such specials as grilled salmon and smoked-bacon green beans. Fried green tomatoes are filled with herb cream cheese, and a pecan pie is made with bourbon and imported Belgian dark chocolate. The airy, curving dining room has white honeycomb windows and an unusual ceiling ornamentation of bronze ribbons. 950 15th St. NW, Downtown, tel. 202/393–4499. AE, D, DC, MC, V. No lunch Sat. Metro: McPherson Square.

Spanish

$$–$$$$ JALEO. ★ You are encouraged to make a meal of the long list of tapas at this lively Spanish bistro, although entrées like grilled fish and paella are just as tasty. Tapas highlights are *gambas al ajillo* (sautéed garlic shrimp), fried potatoes with spicy tomato sauce, and *pinchitos* (a skewer of grilled chorizo) with garlic mashed potatoes. Don't miss the crisp apple Charlotte and the chocolate hazelnut torte. Live flamenco dancing heats up the restaurant on Wednesdays. 480 7th St. NW, Downtown, tel. 202/628–7949. Metro: Gallery Place/Chinatown. AE, D, DC, MC, V.

$$$ TABERNA DEL ALABARDERO. ★ A lovely formal dining room, skillful service, and sophisticated cooking make this restaurant one of Washington's best. Start with tapas: piquillo peppers stuffed with *bacalao* (salted cod) or roasted leg of duck in a phyllo pastry pouch. Proceed to a hefty bowl of gazpacho or white garlic soup and venture on to authentic paella and elegant Spanish country dishes. Ask the sommelier to pick a good Spanish wine to accompany your meal. The plush decor and handsome bar create a romantic atmosphere that attracts a well-heeled clientele. *1776 I St. NW, at 18th St., Downtown, tel. 202/429–2200. Reservations essential. Jacket required. AE, D, DC, MC, V. Closed Sun. No lunch Sat. Metro: Farragut West.*

DUPONT CIRCLE

American/Casual

$$ KRAMERBOOKS AND AFTERWORDS. A favorite neighborhood breakfast spot, this popular bookstore-cum-café is also a late-night haunt on weekends, when it's open around the clock. There's a simple menu with soups, salads, and sandwiches, but many people drop in just for cappuccino and dessert. The dysfunctional family sundae—a massive brownie soaked in amaretto with a plethora of divine toppings—is a local favorite. Live music, from rock to blues, is performed Wednesday through Sunday 10 PM to midnight. *1517 Connecticut Ave. NW, Dupont Circle, tel. 202/387–1462. Reservations not accepted. AE, D, MC, V. Metro: Dupont Circle.*

Asian

$–$$ CITY LIGHTS OF CHINA. The traditional Chinese fare and art-deco design at City Lights have made it a consistent pick on critics' lists. Less common specialties are shark's-fin soup and lamb in a tangy peppery sauce. Seafood items tend to be costly, but there are plenty of reasonably priced alternatives. For satisfying and inexpensive one-dish meals try the pickled-mustard-green soup with noodles and pork, or the *cha chang mein*, the Chinese counterpart to spaghetti with meat sauce. The mint-green booths and elegant silk-flower arrangements conjure up breezy spring days, even in the midst of a frenzied dinner rush. *1731 Connecticut Ave. NW, Dupont Circle, tel. 202/265–6688. AE, D, DC, MC, V. Metro: Dupont Circle.*

$–$$ SALA THAI. Who says Thai food has to be scalp-sweating hot? Sala Thai makes the food as spicy as you wish, but the chef is interested in flavor, not fire. Among the subtly seasoned dishes are *panang goong* (shrimp in curry–peanut sauce), chicken sautéed with ginger and pineapple, and flounder with a choice of four sauces. Mirrored walls and warm lights soften this small downstairs dining room, as do the friendly service and largely neighborhood clientele. *2016 P St. NW, Dupont Circle, tel. 202/872–1144. AE, D, DC, MC, V. Metro: Dupont Circle.*

Contemporary

$$$ NORA. Although it bills itself as an "organic restaurant," Nora is no collective-run juice bar. The food, like the quilt-decorated dining room, is sophisticated and attractive. Peppered beef carpaccio with Manchego cheese is a good starter. Entrées such as seared rockfish with artichoke broth, grilled lamb chops with white-bean *ragù* (sauce), and risotto with winter vegetables emphasize well-balanced, complex ingredients. *2132 Florida Ave. NW, Dupont Circle, tel. 202/462–5143. Reservations essential. AE, D, MC, V. Closed Sun. No lunch. Metro: Dupont Circle.*

French

$–$$$ BISTROT DU COIN. An instant hit in its Dupont Circle neighborhood, this moderately priced French steak house is noisy, crowded, and great fun. The brainchild of Michel Verdon (formerly of Les Halles) and chef Yannis Felix has a monumental zinc bar and serves comforting traditional bistro fare. Mussels, as a starter, come in any of several preparations. Steaks, garnished with a pile of crisp fries, are the main attraction, but you might also try the duck-leg confit or tripe *à la niçoise* (a stew of tripe and fresh tomatoes). Wash it all down with a carafe of Beaujolais or Côtes du Rhone, or with a pitcher of Alsatian white. *1738 Connecticut Ave. NW, Dupont Circle, tel. 202/234–6969. AE, D, DC, MC, V. Metro: Dupont Circle.*

Italian

$$–$$$$ ★ **I RICCHI.** An airy space with terra-cotta tiles, cream-color archways, and floral frescoes, i Ricchi remains a favorite of critics and upscale crowds for its earthy Tuscan cuisine, often prepared on its wood-burning grill or oven. Skewered shrimp and rolled pork roasted in wine and fresh herbs highlight the spring–summer menu. The fall–winter bill of fare brings grilled lamb chops, thick soups, and sautéed beef filet. *1220 19th St. NW, Dupont Circle, tel. 202/835–0459. Reservations essential. Jacket required. AE, DC, MC, V. Closed Sun. No lunch Sat. Metro: Dupont Circle.*

$–$$ **PIZZERIA PARADISO.** The ever popular Pizzeria Paradiso sticks to crowd-pleasing basics: pizzas, *panini* (sandwiches such as Italian cured ham and sun-dried tomatoes and basil), salads, and desserts. Although the standard pizza is satisfying, you can enliven things by ordering it with fresh buffalo mozzarella or unusual toppings such as potatoes, capers, and mussels. The intensely flavored gelato is a house specialty. A trompe l'oeil ceiling adds space and light to a simple interior. *2029 P St. NW, Dupont Circle, tel. 202/223–1245. Reservations not accepted. DC, MC, V. Metro: Dupont Circle.*

Latin American

$$–$$$ **GABRIEL.** Traditional Latin American and Spanish dishes get a nouvelle approach at Gabriel. *Pupusas,* Salvadoran meat patties, are filled with chorizo; appetizer sea scallops are grilled and served with lime, cilantro, and garlic cream. An extensive tapas buffet makes the bar a popular after-work hangout. The restaurant comes into its own with an outstanding Sunday brunch buffet, where you choose from whole suckling pig, made-to-order quesadillas, and Mediterranean specialties like paella and cassoulet, in addition to traditional breakfast items. *Radisson Barceló Hotel, 2121 P St. NW, Dupont Circle, tel. 202/956–6690. Reservations essential. AE, D, DC, MC, V. No lunch Sat. Metro: Dupont Circle.*

Middle Eastern

$–$$ SKEWERS/CAFÉ LUNA. As the name implies, the focus at Skewers is on kabobs, here served with almond-flaked rice or pasta. Lamb with eggplant and chicken with roasted pepper are the most popular variations, but vegetable kabobs and skewers of filet mignon and seasonal seafood are equally tasty. With nearly 20 choices, the appetizer selection is huge. If the restaurant is too crowded, you can enjoy the cheap eats (chicken and avocado salad, mozzarella and tomato sandwiches, vegetable lasagna, pizza, and salads) downstairs at Café Luna or the reading room—coffeehouse upstairs at Luna Books. *1633 P St. NW, Dupont Circle, tel. 202/387–7400 Skewers; 202/387–4005 Café Luna. AE, D, DC, MC, V. Metro: Dupont Circle.*

Seafood

$$–$$$ JOHNNY'S HALF SHELL. It's almost always crowded, but Johnny's Half Shell is worth the wait. Owners John Fulchino and Ann Cashion (both of Cashion's Eat Place in Woodley Park) have created a modern version of the traditional mid-Atlantic seafood house, where you can be comfortable ordering oysters on the half shell and a beer at the bar or settling into one of the roomy booths for a first course of the best fried oysters in town followed by local rockfish or broiled lobster. *2002 P St. NW, Dupont Circle, tel. 202/296–2021. Reservations not accepted. AE, MC, V. Closed Sun. Metro: Dupont Circle.*

Steak

$$–$$$ **PALM.** A favorite lunchtime hangout of power brokers, the Palm has walls papered with caricatures of the famous patrons who have dined here. Main attractions include gargantuan steaks and Nova Scotia lobsters, several kinds of potatoes, and New York cheesecake. But one of Palm's best-kept secrets is that it's also a terrific, old-fashioned Italian restaurant. Try the veal marsala for lunch or, on Thursday, the terrific shrimp in marinara sauce. *1225 19th St. NW, Dupont Circle, tel. 202/293–9091. Reservations essential. AE, D, DC, MC, V. No lunch weekends. Metro: Dupont Circle.*

GEORGETOWN/WEST END/GLOVER PARK

American

$$$ **PALENA.** Chef Frank Ruta and pastry chef Ann Amernick met while working in the White House kitchens; now they've joined forces to open this contemporary American restaurant named for the Italian village where Ruta's great-grandmother lived. The French-, Italian-, and American-influenced menu changes seasonally. Sometimes Amernick and Ruta team up, as for an appetizer of crisp puff pastry with fresh sardines and greens. Ruta goes it alone with a veal chop with a barley-stuffed pepper and a pork chop with flavorful baked beans. *3529 Connecticut Ave. NW, Cleveland Park, tel. 202/537–9250. AE, D, DC, MC, V. Closed Sun. No lunch. Metro: Cleveland Park.*

$ **GEORGETOWN CAFÉ.** With its unpretentious decor, cheap prices, and eclectic, lowbrow menu, this café is a bit of a neighborhood oddball. Students and other locals frequent it for the pasta, pizzas, kabobs, gyros, and such home-style American favorites as roast beef, baked chicken, and mashed potatoes. Closed only from 6 to 9 AM weekdays and open 24 hours on weekends, Georgetown Café is also good for a late-night snack. *1623 Wisconsin Ave. NW, Georgetown, tel. 202/333–0215. Reservations not accepted. D, MC, V.*

Asian

$–$$ SUSHI-KO. At the city's best Japanese restaurant, daily specials
★ are always innovative: sesame oil–seasoned trout is layered with
crisp wonton crackers, and a sushi special might be salmon
topped with a touch of mango sauce and a tiny sprig of dill. 2309
*Wisconsin Ave. NW, Georgetown, tel. 202/333–4187. AE, MC, V. No
lunch Sat.–Mon.*

Contemporary

$$$$ CITRONELLE. See all the action in the glass-front kitchen at chef
★ Michel Richard's flagship California–French restaurant. Witty
appetizers might be a "tart" of thinly sliced grilled scallops or
"beignets" of foie gras coated with *kataife* (a grain that resembles
shredded wheat) and deep-fried. Main courses could be loin of
venison with chestnuts, mushrooms, and wine sauce or a breast
of squab with truffle sauce. A chef's table in the kitchen gives lucky
diners (who have made reservations at least a month in advance)
a ringside seat. A prix-fixe menu ranges from $95 to $150. *Latham
Hotel, 3000 M St. NW, Georgetown, tel. 202/625–2150. Reservations
essential. Jacket required. AE, D, DC, MC, V.*

$$–$$$$ 1789. This elegant dining room, with Early American paintings and
★ a fireplace, could easily be a room in the White House. But proper
and genteel decor is offset by down-to-earth food. Soups, such
as the seafood stew and the rich black bean soup with unsweetened
chocolate, are flavorful. Rack of lamb and fillet of beef are
specialties, and seared tuna stands out among the excellent
seafood dishes. Service is fluid and attentive. *1226 36th St. NW,
Georgetown, tel. 202/965–1789. Reservations essential. Jacket required.
AE, D, DC, MC, V. No lunch.*

French

$$–$$$ BISTRO FRANÇAIS. Washington's chefs head to Bistro Français
for its minute steak maître d'hôtel or the sirloin with black pepper

or red wine sauce. For many, the big draw is the rotisserie chicken. Daily specials may include *suprême* of salmon with broccoli mousse and beurre blanc. The restaurant is divided into two parts—the café side and the more formal dining room; the café menu has sandwiches and omelets in addition to entrées. The Bistro also has fixed-price lunches ($15.95), early and late-night dinner specials ($18.95), and all-you-can-eat brunches on weekends ($16.95). It stays open until 3 AM Sunday through Thursday, 4 AM Friday and Saturday. *3128 M St. NW, Georgetown, tel. 202/338–3830. AE, DC, MC, V.*

Indian

$–$$ HERITAGE INDIA. You feel like a guest in a foreign land dining at this restaurant that gives incredible attention to detail in everything from the tapestried chairs to the paintings of India to the traditional tandoori and curry dishes. *Tahli* (a variety plate, with rice, bread, and six or seven curries or meats separated into small bowls or compartments) is served on a silver platter with rice, lamb, chicken, and curries; the wine is presented in a small glass pitcher. Whatever you choose, the experience is as fascinating as the meal. *2400 Wisconsin Ave. NW, Glover Park, tel. 202/333–3120. AE, D, MC, V.*

Italian

$$–$$$$ CAFE MILANO. You're likely to rub shoulders with local socialites, sports figures, and visiting celebrities at Cafe Milano's crowded bar. Expect authentic, sophisticated Italian cooking and a pricey wine list. Specialties are pasta dishes like the elegant lobster with linguine, composed salads, and light-crust pizzas. *3251 Prospect St. NW, Georgetown, tel. 202/333–6183. AE, D, DC, MC, V.*

$–$$ TWO AMYS. Judging from the long lines here, the best pizza in D.C. may have moved uptown. Simple recipes allow the ingredients to speak for themselves at this Neapolitan pizzeria. It's no surprise

Eating Well Is the Best Revenge

Eating out is a major part of every travel experience. It's a chance to explore flavors you don't find at home. And often the walking you do on vacation means that you can dig in without guilt.

START AT THE TOP By all means take in a really good restaurant or two while you're on the road. A trip is a time to kick back and savor the pleasures of the palate. Read up on the culinary scene before you leave home. Check out representative menus on the Web—some chefs have gone electronic. And ask friends who have just come back. Then reserve a table as far in advance as you can, remembering that the best establishments book up months in advance. Remember that some good restaurants require you to reconfirm the day before or the day of your meal. Then again, some really good places will call you, so make sure to leave a number where you can be reached.

ADVENTURES IN EATING A trip is the perfect opportunity to try food you can't get at home. So leave yourself open to try an ethnic food that's not represented where you live or to eat fruits and vegetables you've never heard of. One of them may become your next favorite food.

BEYOND GUIDEBOOKS You can rely on the restaurants you find in these pages. But also look for restaurants on your own. When you're ready for lunch, ask people you meet where they eat. Look for tiny holes-in-the-wall with a loyal following and the best burgers or crispiest pizza crust. Find out about local chains whose fame rests upon a single memorable dish. There's hardly a food-lover who doesn't relish the chance to share a favorite place. It's fun to come up with your own special find—and asking about food is a great way to start a conversation.

SAMPLE LOCAL FLAVORS Do check out the specialties. Is there a special brand of ice cream or a special dish that you simply must try?

HAVE A PICNIC Every so often eat al fresco. Grocery shopping gives you a whole different view of a place.

that Peter Pastan, owner of fine Italian restaurant Obelisk, is co-owner of this restaurant. You can taste his high standards in every bite. You may be tempted to go for the D.O.C. pizza (approved by the *Denominazione di Origine Controllata* as having authentic Neopolitan ingredients and methods of preparation), but don't hesitate to try the daily specials. This place is very child-friendly. *3715 Macomb St. NW, Glover Park, tel. 202/885–5700. Reservations not accepted. MC, V.*

In This Chapter

Updated by Robin Dougherty and Karyn-Siobhan Robinson

shopping

AFRICAN MASKS LIKE THOSE that inspired Picasso; kitchenware as objets d'art; bargains on apparel by Christian Dior, Hugo Boss, and Burberry; paisley scarves from India; American and European antiques; books of every description; handicrafts from almost two dozen Native American tribes; music boxes by the thousands; busts of U.S. presidents; textiles by the score; fine leather goods—all this and more can be found in the nation's capital.

Sales tax is 6%, and major credit cards and traveler's checks are accepted virtually everywhere. Each shop's listing below includes the nearest Metro station, although some may be as far as a 15- to 20-minute walk; we do not list Metro stops for the few stores that have no Metro within walking distance.

ADAMS-MORGAN

Scattered among the dozens of Latin, Ethiopian, and Caribbean restaurants in this most bohemian of Washington neighborhoods are a score of eccentric shops. If quality is what you seek, **ADAMS-MORGAN** and nearby Woodley Park can be a minefield; tread cautiously. Still, for the bargain hunter it's great fun. If bound for a specific shop, you may wish to call ahead to verify hours. Adams-Morganites are often not clock-watchers, although you can be sure an afternoon stroll on the weekend will find a good representation of the shops open and give you a few hours of great browsing. *18th St. NW, between Columbia Rd. and Florida Ave., Adams-Morgan. Metro: Woodley Park/Zoo or Dupont Circle.*

Specialty Stores

ANTIQUES AND COLLECTIBLES

CHENONCEAU ANTIQUES. The mostly American 19th- and 20th-century pieces on this shop's two floors were selected by a buyer with an exquisite eye. Merchandise includes beautiful 19th-century paisley scarves from India and Scotland, and 1920s glass lamps. *2314 18th St. NW, Woodley Park, tel. 202/667–1651. Closed weekdays. Metro: Woodley Park/Zoo.*

MISS PIXIE'S. Two levels of well-chosen collectibles include gorgeous parasols and umbrellas, antique home furnishings, glass- and silverware, vintage clothes, and hardwood bed frames. The low prices should keep your attention. *1810 Adams Mill Rd. NW, Adams-Morgan, tel. 202/232–8171. Closed Mon.–Wed. Metro: Woodley Park/Zoo.*

BOOKS

IDLE TIME BOOKS. This used bookstore sells "rare to medium rare" books with plenty of meaty titles in all genres, especially out-of-print literature. *2410 18th St. NW, Woodley Park, tel. 202/232–4774. Metro: Woodley Park/Zoo.*

YAWA. Along with a large collection of African and African-American fiction and nonfiction, magazines, and children's books, Yawa also sells ethnic jewelry, crafts, and greeting cards. *2206 18th St. NW, Adams-Morgan, tel. 202/483–6805. Metro: Dupont Circle.*

CLOTHING

KHISMET WEARABLE ART SHOWROOM. Owner Millée Spears fills her colorful shop with traditional women's garments from West Africa as well as her own original designs. Spears, who lived in Ghana, uses ethnic-print fabrics to create garments that are suitable for both work and an evening out and will custom design if desired. *1800 Belmont Rd. NW, Adams-Morgan, tel. 202/678–4499. Open weekends and by appointment. Metro: Dupont Circle.*

KOBOS. Those looking to add traditional ethnic dress to their wardrobe may appreciate this shop's rainbow of clothing and accessories, all imported from West Africa. *2444 18th St. NW, Adams-Morgan, tel. 202/332–9580. Metro: Woodley Park/Zoo.*

NIAGARA. Tucked inside the DC CD music store, this compact boutique offers ultrahip vintage and contemporary clothes. *2423 18th St. NW, Woodley Park, tel. 202/332–7474. Closed Tues. Metro: Woodley Park/Zoo.*

MUSIC
DC CD. The club crowd loves this upstart music store, which has late hours and a wide selection of indie, rock, hip-hop, alternative, and soul. The knowledgeable staff often opens packages, allowing customers to listen before they buy. *2423 18th St. NW, Adams-Morgan, tel. 202/588–1810. Metro: Woodley Park/Zoo.*

SHOES
SHAKE YOUR BOOTY. Trend-conscious Washingtonians come here for modish leather boots and platform shoes. *2324 18th St. NW, Adams-Morgan, tel. 202/518–8205. Closed Tues. Metro: Woodley Park/Zoo.*

CAPITOL HILL/EASTERN MARKET
As the Capitol Hill area has become gentrified, unique shops and boutiques have sprung up, many clustered around the redbrick structure of **EASTERN MARKET.** Inside are produce and meat counters, plus the Market Five art gallery; outside are a farmers' market (on Saturday) and a flea market (on weekends). Along 7th Street you'll find a number of small shops, selling everything from art books to handwoven rugs to antiques and knickknacks. *7th and C Sts. SE, Capitol Hill. Metro: Eastern Market, Union Station, or Capitol South.*

Mall

UNION STATION. This delightful shopping enclave, resplendent with marble floors and gilded, vaulted ceilings, is inside a working train station. You'll find several familiar retailers, including Jones New York, Aerosole, Swatch, and Ann Taylor, as well as a bookstore and a multiplex cinema. The east hall, reminiscent of London's Covent Garden, is filled with vendors of expensive and ethnic wares in open stalls. Christmas is an especially pleasant time to shop here. *50 Massachusetts Ave. NE, Capitol Hill, tel. 202/371–9441, www.unionstationdc.com. Metro: Union Station.*

Specialty Stores

ANTIQUES AND COLLECTIBLES
ANTIQUES ON THE HILL. This store has the feel of an old thrift shop where nothing is ever thrown away. From floor to roof, knickknacks of every kind fill the shelves. The center of the floor is filled with furniture, and light fixtures hang from every available spot on the ceiling. *701 North Carolina Ave. SE, Capitol Hill, tel. 202/543–1819. Closed Mon.–Tues. Metro: Eastern Market.*

BOOKS
BIRD-IN-HAND BOOKSTORE AND GALLERY. This quirky store specializes in books on art and design and also carries exhibition catalogs. *323 7th St. SE, Capitol Hill, tel. 202/543–0744. Closed Sun.–Mon. Metro: Eastern Market.*

CAPITOL HILL BOOKS. Pop into this inviting store to browse through a wonderful collection of out-of-print history books and modern first editions. *657 C St. SE, Capitol Hill, tel. 202/544–1621. Metro: Eastern Market.*

CLOTHING
THE FORECAST. If you favor classic, contemporary styles, Forecast should be in your future. It sells women's silk sweaters

and wool blends in solid, muted tones that won't quickly fall out of fashion. *218 7th St. SE, Eastern Market, tel. 202/547–7337. Closed Mon. Metro: Eastern Market.*

CRAFTS AND GIFTS

WOVEN HISTORY/SILK ROAD. These connected stores sell handmade treasures from small villages around the world. Silk Road sells home furnishings, gifts, clothing, collectible rugs, and accessories made in Asian mountain communities as well as such contemporary items as aromatherapy candles from not-so-rural Greenwich Village in New York. Woven History's rugs are made the old-fashioned way, with vegetable dyes and hand-spun wool. *311–315 7th St. SE, Capitol Hill, tel. 202/543–1705. Metro: Eastern Market.*

DOWNTOWN

The domain of the city's many office workers, downtown tends to shut down at 5 PM sharp with the exception of the larger department stores. **OLD DOWNTOWN** is where you'll find **Hecht's** (1201 G St. NW) department store and sundry specialty stores; established chains such as Ann Taylor and Gap tend to be concentrated near Farragut Square. Avoid the lunch-hour crowds to ensure more leisurely shopping. *North of Pennsylvania Ave. between 7th and 18th Sts., up to Connecticut Ave. below L St., Downtown. Metro: Archives/Navy Memorial, Farragut North and West, Foggy Bottom/GWU, Gallery Place, McPherson Square, or Metro Center.*

Mall

SHOPS AT NATIONAL PLACE. The Shops takes up three levels, one devoted entirely to food stands. It's mainly youth-oriented (this is a good place to drop off teenagers weary of the Smithsonian and more in the mood to buy T-shirts), but Perfumania and clothing stores such as Casual Corner and August Max have branches here, too. Those in search of presidential souvenirs may find the White House Gift Shop quite handy. *13th and F Sts. NW, Downtown, tel. 202/662–1250. Metro: Metro Center.*

Specialty Stores

ART GALLERIES

NUMARK GALLERY. This powerhouse gallery brings in established and cutting-edge artists: Peter Halley, Tony Feher, and Michal Rovner have shown their works here. International, national, and regional artists are also regularly featured. *406 7th St. NW, Chinatown, tel. 202/628–3810. Metro: Gallery Place/Chinatown.*

THE TOUCHSTONE GALLERY. Minimalist paintings and photography are showcased at this gallery. *406 7th St. NW, Chinatown, tel. 202/347–2787. Metro: Gallery Place/Chinatown.*

ZENITH GALLERY. Founded in 1978, the Zenith exhibits indoor and outdoor sculpture, mixed media, wearable art, jewelry, crafts, and art furniture, as well as a large selection of paintings by national and international artists. *413 7th St. NW, Chinatown, tel. 202/783–2963. Metro: Gallery Place/Chinatown.*

BOOKS

CHAPTERS. This "literary bookstore" fills its shelves with serious contemporary fiction, classics, foreign language titles, and poetry. The store hosts author readings regularly, so check the schedule if you're spending a few days in town. *1512 K St. NW, Downtown, tel. 202/347–5495. Metro: McPherson Square.*

OLSSONS BOOKS AND RECORDS. The store stocks a large and varied collection of books for readers of all ages and a good selection of classical and folk music. Hours vary significantly from store to store. In addition to the downtown locations, there's a branch in Dupont Circle. *1200 F St. NW, Downtown, tel. 202/347–3686; Metro: Metro Center. 418 7th St. NW, Downtown, tel. 202/638–7610; Metro: Archives/Navy Memorial.*

CLOTHING

BRITCHES OF GEORGETOWN. The larger of two Washington branches (the other is in Georgetown), this store has a wide selection of traditional but trend-conscious men's clothing. In addition to the store's private label, you'll find menswear by St. Andrews and Hickey Freeman. *1776 K St. NW, Downtown, tel. 202/ 347–8994. Metro: Farragut North.*

BROOKS BROTHERS. This venerable clothier has been issuing its discreet label since 1818. Men with classic tastes—gray wool suits; navy blazers; chinos; dignified formal wear; and of course the original, glorious cotton dress shirt—can always take comfort here. And these days, so can women, with a selection of classic casual and work clothes for her. *1201 Connecticut Ave. NW, Downtown, tel. 202/659–4650. Metro: Farragut North.*

BURBERRY. Burberry made its reputation with the still-popular trench coat, but this British company also manufactures traditional men's and women's indoor apparel and accessories. *1155 Connecticut Ave. NW, Downtown, tel. 202/463–3000. Metro: Farragut North.*

CHANEL BOUTIQUE. The Willard Hotel annex is the place to find handbags, perfume, couture women's fashions, and other goodies from this legendary house of fashion. *1455 Pennsylvania Ave. NW, Downtown, tel. 202/638–5055. Metro: Metro Center.*

EARL ALLEN. Earl Allen offers conservative but distinctive dresses and sportswear for women, wearable art, and one-of-a-kind items—much of it made exclusively for this store. *1825 I St. NW, Downtown, tel. 202/466–3437. Closed weekends. Metro: Farragut West.*

J. PRESS. Like its flagship store, founded in Connecticut in 1902 as a custom shop for Yale University, this Washington outlet is a resolutely traditional clothier: Shetland and Irish wool sport coats are a specialty. *1801 L St. NW, Downtown, tel. 202/857–0120. Metro: Farragut North.*

RIZIK BROS. This Washington institution offers both designer clothing and expert advice for women. The sales staff is trained to find just the right style from the store's inventory. Take the elevator up from the northwest corner of Connecticut Avenue and L Street. *1100 Connecticut Ave. NW, Downtown, tel. 202/223–4050. Metro: Farragut North.*

CRAFTS AND GIFTS

AL'S MAGIC SHOP. For professional magicians, aspiring kids, and amateur pranksters, Al's has offered a full line of cards, tricks, magic wands, and mind games for more than 65 years. Original proprietor Al Cohen counted Doug Henning and David Copperfield among his customers. Since Al's retirement in 2002, a new owner has kept this Washington landmark alive. *1012 Vermont Ave. NW, Downtown, tel. 202/789–2800. Metro: McPherson Square.*

INDIAN CRAFT SHOP. Handicrafts, such as jewelry, pottery, sand paintings, weavings, and baskets from more than 45 Native American tribes range from inexpensive (as little as $5) jewelry on up to collector-quality art pieces (more than $1,000). You need a photo ID to enter the federal building. *Department of the Interior, 1849 C St. NW, Room 1023, Downtown, tel. 202/208–4056. Closed weekends. Metro: Farragut West.*

JEWELRY

PAMPILLONIA JEWELERS. Here you'll find traditional designs in 18-karat gold and platinum as well as eye-catching contemporary designs. The selection for men is particularly good. *1213 Connecticut Ave. NW, Downtown, tel. 202/628–6305. Metro: Farragut North.*

TINY JEWEL BOX. Despite its name, this shop offers three floors of precious and semi-precious wares, including works by well-known designers and unique gifts. *1147 Connecticut Ave. NW, Downtown, tel. 202/393–2747. Metro: Farragut North.*

SHOES

CHURCH'S. Church's is a top-notch English company whose handmade men's shoes are noted for their comfort and durability. 1820 L St. NW, Downtown, tel. 202/296–3366. Metro: Farragut North.

DUPONT CIRCLE

You might call **DUPONT CIRCLE** a younger, hipper version of Georgetown—almost as pricey and not quite as well kept, with more apartment buildings than houses. Its many restaurants, offbeat shops, and specialty book and record stores lend it a distinctive, cosmopolitan air. The street scene here is more urban than Georgetown's, with bike messengers and chess aficionados filling up the park while shoppers frequent the many coffee shops and stores. Connecticut Ave. between M and S Sts.. Metro: Dupont Circle.

Specialty Stores

ANTIQUES AND COLLECTIBLES

GEOFFREY DINER GALLERY. This shop is a must for hard-core antiques shoppers on the hunt for 19th-century wares, including Tiffany lamps and Arts and Crafts pieces from England and the U.S. 1730 21st St. NW, Dupont Circle, tel. 202/483–5005. Metro: Dupont Circle.

ART GALLERIES

On "First Fridays," the joint open house held on the first Friday of each month, the streets are filled with wine-and-cheese–loving gallery hoppers. Check out **THE GALLERIES OF DUPONT CIRCLE** (www.artgalleriesdc.com) for information on all events.

AMERICA, OH YES! Home to one of the most extensive folk art collections in the country, this gallery is known for its reasonable prices. 1700 Connecticut Ave. NW, Suite 300, Dupont Circle, tel. 202/483–9644. Metro: Dupont Circle.

BURDICK GALLERY. John Burdick's cozy gallery focuses on Inuit art and sculpture and works on paper by Canadian Eskimos. *1609 Connecticut Ave. NW, Dupont Circle, tel. 202/986–5682. Metro: Dupont Circle.*

BURTON MARINKOVICH FINE ART. This gallery has works on paper by modern and contemporary masters, including Bleckner, Kandinsky, Matisse, Motherwell, Picasso, and others. Rare modern illustrated books and British linocuts from the Grosvenor School are also specialties. *1506 21st St. NW, Dupont Circle, tel. 202/296–6563. Metro: Dupont Circle.*

GALLERY K. H. Marc Moyens and Komei Wachi have devoted a lifetime to amassing a sizeable collection of contemporary art. Their spacious gallery holds a large inventory, including such internationally known artists as Andy Warhol, Robert Motherwell, and Jackson Pollock. *2010 R St. NW, Dupont Circle, tel. 202/234–0339. Metro: Dupont Circle.*

BOOKS

KRAMERBOOKS AND AFTERWORDS. One of Washington's best loved independents, this cozy shop with a café has a choice selection of fiction and nonfiction. Open 24 hours on weekends, it's a convenient meeting place. *1517 Connecticut Ave. NW, Dupont Circle, tel. 202/387–1400, www.kramers.com. Metro: Dupont Circle.*

LAMBDA RISING. A major player in the Dupont Circle area, Lambda features novels by gay and lesbian writers and other books of interest to the gay community. *1625 Connecticut Ave. NW, Dupont Circle, tel. 202/462–6969. Metro: Dupont Circle.*

OLSSONS BOOKS AND RECORDS. Like its sister stores Downtown, this branch prides itself on its wide selection of books and music. *1307 19th St. NW, Dupont Circle, tel. 202/785–1133. Metro: Dupont Circle.*

CLOTHING

BETSY FISHER. Catering to women of all ages in search of contemporary styles, this store stocks one-of-a-kind accessories, duds, and jewelry. *1224 Connecticut Ave. NW, tel. 202/ 785–1975. Metro: Dupont Circle (south exit).*

KID'S CLOSET. If filling a little one's closet is on your list, stop here for quality contemporary children's clothing and toys. *1226 Connecticut Ave. NW, Dupont Circle, tel. 202/429–9247. Metro: Dupont Circle (south exit).*

SECONDI. The city's finest consignment shop, Secondi's well-chosen selection of women's designer and casual clothing, accessories, and shoes includes labels such as Donna Karan, Prada, Ann Taylor, and Coach. *1702 Connecticut Ave. NW, Dupont Circle, tel. 202/667–1122. Metro: Dupont Circle.*

CONFECTIONS

THE CHOCOLATE MOOSE. The place to stop if you're looking for the perfect molded chocolate or hand-made treat. The store carries its own wares as well as those of premium chocolatiers. *1800 M St. NW, Dupont Circle, tel. 202/463–0992. Metro: Dupont Circle.*

CRAFTS AND GIFTS

BEADAZZLED. This appealing shop stocks a dazzling number of ready-to-string beads and jewelry as well as books on crafts history and techniques. *1507 Connecticut Ave. NW, Dupont Circle, tel. 202/265–2323, www.beadazzled.net. Metro: Dupont Circle.*

SHOES

SHOE SCENE. The fashionable, moderately priced shoes for women found here are imported from Europe. *1330 Connecticut Ave. NW, Dupont Circle, tel. 202/659–2194. Metro: Dupont Circle.*

GEORGETOWN

Washington's favorite shopping area, **GEORGETOWN** is the capital's center for famous citizens, as well as for restaurants, bars, nightclubs, and trendy shops. Although Georgetown is not on a subway line (the nearest Metro, Foggy Bottom/GWU, is a 10- to 15-minute walk from the shops) and parking is difficult at best, people still flock here. National chains are beginning to overtake the specialty shops that first gave the district its allure, but the historic neighborhood is still charming, and its street scene lively. In addition to housing tony antiques, elegant crafts, and high-style shoe and clothing boutiques, Georgetown offers wares that attract local college students and young people: books, music, and fashions from familiar names like Banana Republic and Urban Outfitters. Most stores lie to the east and west on M Street and to the north on Wisconsin. *Intersection of Wisconsin Ave. and M St., Georgetown. Metro: Foggy Bottom/GWU.*

Mall

THE SHOPS AT GEORGETOWN PARK, near the hub of the Georgetown shopping district, at the intersection of Wisconsin Avenue and M Street, is a posh tri-level mall, which looks like a Victorian ice-cream parlor inside. The pricey clothing and accessory boutiques and the ubiquitous chain stores (such as Victoria's Secret), as well as the upscale Sharper Image, draw international visitors in droves. Next door is a branch of Dean & Deluca, the gourmet food store. *3222 M St. NW, Georgetown, tel. 202/298–5577. Metro: Foggy Bottom/GWU.*

Specialty Stores

ANTIQUES AND COLLECTIBLES

GEORGETOWN ANTIQUES CENTER. The center, in a Victorian town house, has two dealers who share space: Cherub Gallery specializes in art nouveau and art deco, and Michael Getz

Antiques sells fireplace equipment and silverware. 2918 M St. NW, Georgetown, tel. 202/337–2224 Cherub Gallery; 202/338–3811 Michael Getz Antiques. Metro: Foggy Bottom/GWU.

MILLER & ARNEY ANTIQUES. English, American, and European furniture and accessories from the 17th, 18th, and early 19th centuries give Miller & Arney Antiques a museum-gallery air. Asian porcelain adds splashes of color. 1737 Wisconsin Ave. NW, Georgetown, tel. 202/338–2369. Metro: Foggy Bottom/GWU.

OLD PRINT GALLERY. Here you'll find the capital's largest collection of old prints, with a focus on maps and 19th-century decorative prints (including Washingtoniana). 1220 31st St. NW, Georgetown, tel. 202/965–1818. Closed Sun. Metro: Foggy Bottom/GWU.

SUSQUEHANNA. With three rooms upstairs, four rooms downstairs, and a garden full of benches, urns, and tables, Susquehanna is the largest antiques shop in Georgetown. American and English furniture is the specialty. 3216 O St. NW, Georgetown, tel. 202/333–1511. Metro: Foggy Bottom/GWU.

ART GALLERIES
ADDISON RIPLEY. This well-respected gallery exhibits contemporary work by local artists, including painters Manon Cleary and Wolf Kahn and photographer Terri Weifenbach. 1670 Wisconsin Ave. NW, Georgetown, tel. 202/338–5180. Metro: Foggy Bottom/GWU.

CREIGHTON-DAVIS. Collectors with deep pockets can pick up a Matisse at this art powerhouse, which has also been known to carry Whistlers. Georgetown Park Mall, 3222 M St. NW, Georgetown, tel. 202/333–3050. Metro: Foggy Bottom/GWU.

GALLERIES 1054. Six distinct, mostly contemporary, galleries live under one roof here. 1054 31st St. NW, Georgetown. Metro: Foggy Bottom/GWU.

SPECTRUM. Thirty artists form this cooperative gallery, which specializes in abstract and representational art. 1132 29th St. NW, Georgetown, tel. 202/333–0954. Metro: Foggy Bottom/GWU.

BOOKS

BRIDGE STREET BOOKS. This charming bookshop stocks a good selection of literature as well as books on fine arts, politics, and other subjects. 2814 Pennsylvania Ave. NW, Georgetown, tel. 202/965–5200. Metro: Foggy Bottom/GWU.

CLOTHING

BETSEY JOHNSON. The fanciful frocks here are favorites of the young and the restless. 1319 Wisconsin Ave. NW, Georgetown, tel. 202/338–4090. Metro: Foggy Bottom/GWU.

BRITCHES OF GEORGETOWN. The smaller of two branches, with the other downtown, this Britches carries an extensive selection of traditional but trend-conscious designs in natural fibers for men. 1245 Wisconsin Ave. NW, Georgetown, tel. 202/338–3330. Metro: Foggy Bottom/GWU.

COMMANDER SALAMANDER. This funky outpost sells trendy clothes for the alternative set—punk kids and ravers. Sifting through the assortment of leather, chains, toys, and candy-color makeup is as much entertainment as it is shopping. The store is open 'til 10 PM on weekends. 1420 Wisconsin Ave. NW, Georgetown, tel. 202/337–2265. Metro: Foggy Bottom/GWU.

PHOENIX. Here you'll find contemporary women's clothing in natural fibers by designers such as Eileen Fisher and Flax, as well as jewelry and art pieces (fine and folk) from Mexico. 1514 Wisconsin Ave. NW, Georgetown, tel. 202/338–4404.

CRAFTS AND GIFTS

AMERICAN STUDIO. One-of-a-kind functional and nonfunctional pieces fill this wonderful place—tea kettles, corkscrews, glassware, and jewelry—all by international designers. 2906 M St. NW, Georgetown, tel. 202/965–3273. Metro: Foggy Bottom/GWU.

APPALACHIAN SPRING. The largest of this chain's four outlets (there are two suburban shops and one in Union Station), Appalachian Spring has a wide selection of traditional and contemporary American-made crafts: jewelry, weavings, pottery, and blown glass. *1415 Wisconsin Ave. NW, Georgetown, tel. 202/337–5780 or 202/682–0505.*

JEWELRY
BLANCA FLOR. The specialty here is elegant, high-quality silver jewelry, mostly from Mexico. *3066 M St. NW, Georgetown, tel. 202/944–5051. Metro: Foggy Bottom/GWU.*

LEATHER GOODS
COACH STORE. Coach carries a complete (and expensive) line of well-made leather handbags, briefcases, belts, and wallets. *1214 Wisconsin Ave. NW, Georgetown, tel. 202/342–1772. Metro: Foggy Bottom/GWU.*

SHOES
PRINCE AND PRINCESS. This retailer carries a full line of men's shoes and boots, including Timberland and Sebago. For women, the selection includes strappy party shoes, chunky platforms, and stylish pumps from designers such as Via Spiga and Nine West. *1400 Wisconsin Ave. NW, Georgetown, tel. 202/337–4211. Metro: Foggy Bottom/GWU.*

SHAKE YOUR BOOTY. The Georgetown location of this Adams-Morgan venue carries trendy, must-have footwear for women who believe that shoes, not diamonds, are a girl's best friend. *3225 M St. NW, Georgetown, tel. 202/333–6524.*

In This Chapter

Updated by Karyn-Siobhan Robinson

nightlife and the arts

THE CAPITAL'S MAIN CLAIM TO FAME has historically been its role as the nation's center of political power. But this one-time cultural desert has become a thriving arts center, home of the National Symphony Orchestra (NSO), the Washington Opera, and the National Theatre. The city plays host to Broadway shows, ballet, modern dance, chamber music series, and military bands. It even has its own "off-Broadway," a half dozen or so plucky theaters scattered around the District.

Much of Washington's nightlife is clustered in key areas. Georgetown has dozens of bars, nightclubs, and restaurants on M Street east and west of Wisconsin Avenue and on Wisconsin Avenue north of M Street. Along the 18th Street strip in Adams-Morgan, bordered by Columbia Road and Florida Avenue, are several small live-music clubs, ethnic restaurants, and bars. The area west of Florida Avenue, along the U Street corridor—perhaps one of the hippest neighborhoods in the country—appeals to young people looking for music from hip-hop to alt-rock. Theatergoers seeking post-show entertainment can check out the 14th Street strip from U Street toward P Street, which has an eclectic, thriving nightlife. A half dozen Capitol Hill bars stretch along Pennsylvania Avenue between 2nd and 4th streets. Last call in D.C. is 2 AM, and most bars and clubs close by 3 AM on the weekends and between midnight and 2 AM during the week.

For calendars of entertainment events, consult Friday's "Weekend" section in the *Washington Post;* its "Guide to the

Lively Arts" is printed daily. On Thursday, look for the *Washington Times* "Weekend" section and the free weekly *Washington CityPaper*. You might also check out the "City Lights" section in the monthly *Washingtonian* magazine. The free *Metro Weekly* and *Women in the Life* magazines offer insights on gay and lesbian nightlife. It's a good idea to call clubs ahead of time to find out what's on. Reservations are advised for comedy clubs; places where reservations are essential are noted.

TICKETS

Tickets to most events are available by calling or visiting each theater's box office, or through the following ticket agencies.

TICKETMASTER (tel. 202/432–7328 or 410/481–7328, www.ticketmaster.com) takes phone charges for many events. You can purchase Ticketmaster tickets in person at all Hecht's department stores. **TICKETPLACE** (Old Post Office Pavilion, 1100 Pennsylvania Ave. NW, Downtown, tel. 202/842–5387), near the Federal Triangle Metro stop, sells half-price, day-of-performance tickets for select shows; a "menu board" lists available performances. There's a 10% service charge per order. TicketPlace is also a full-price Ticketmaster outlet. It's closed on Sunday and Monday; tickets for performances on those days are sold on Saturday. **TICKETS.COM** (tel. 703/218–6500, www.tickets.com) takes reservations for events at Arena Stage, Center Stage, Ford's Theatre, the Holocaust Museum, the 9:30 Club, and Signature Theater. It also has outlets in selected Olsson's Books & Records.

NIGHTLIFE

Acoustic, Folk, and Country Clubs

Washington has a very active folk scene. For information on folk events—from *contra* dancing to storytelling to open singing—

call the recorded information line of the **FOLKLORE SOCIETY OF GREATER WASHINGTON** (tel. 202/546–2228).

SOHO TEA AND COFFEE. Quality singer-songwriters share the stage with poets and writers at Soho's open mike the second and fourth Wednesday of every month, in addition to featured performances on other nights. The café stays open very late and serves breakfast all day, along with its regular menu of light fare. 2150 P St. NW, Dupont Circle, tel. 202/463–7646. Metro: Dupont Circle.

Bars and Lounges

BRICKSKELLER. This is the place to go when you want something more exotic than a Bud Lite. A list of more than 1,000 varieties of beer from around the world earned Brickskeller mention in the 2003 Guinness Book of World Records. Servers actually have to go to "beer school" to land a job here. 1523 22nd St. NW, Dupont Circle, tel. 202/293–1885. Metro: Dupont Circle.

CAP CITY BREWING COMPANY. At the New York Avenue location of this microbrewery, a gleaming copper bar dominates the airy room; metal steps lead up to where the brews—from bitters to bocks—are made. The Postal Square location on Massachusetts Avenue has five 30-keg copper serving vessels in the center of the restaurant. 1100 New York Ave. NW, Downtown, tel. 202/628–2222. Metro: Metro Center; 2 Massachusetts Ave. NE, Capitol Hill, tel. 202/842–2337. Metro: Union Station.

CHI CHA LOUNGE. Stylish young patrons relax on sofas and armchairs, enjoying a menu of Andean appetizers, homemade sangria, and cocktails, while Latin jazz plays in the background. It gets packed on weekends. Sunday through Thursday you can indulge in a Turkish water pipe filled with imported honey-cured tobacco. 1624 U St. NW, U Street, tel. 202/234–8400. Metro: U Street/Cardozo.

EIGHTEENTH STREET LOUNGE (ESL). Yes, it's hard to find. And yes, the guys at the door ARE checking out your clothes, but don't let fear stop you. Fans of techno music flock here, to the home of the ESL record label and the world-renowned DJs, Thievery Corporation. Inside are hardwood floors, candles, and lush couches. 1212 18th St. NW, Dupont Circle, tel. 202/466–3922, www.eslmusic.com. Metro: Dupont Circle.

FADÓ IRISH PUB. Designed by Irish craftsmen with authentic materials, Fadó is really four pubs in one: the Library, the Victorian Pub, the Gaelic, and the Cottage. Live Irish acoustic music is performed every Sunday afternoon, and there's live Celtic rock on Wednesday and Saturday nights. Irish films are shown Monday nights. 808 7th St. NW, Chinatown, tel. 202/789–0066. Metro: Gallery Place/Chinatown.

FELIX. Cool, hip, and chic are the watchwords of the mixed and international crowd that haunts Felix. The sounds of live Latin jazz or funk often waft out to 18th Street. Be sure to sip one of the exotic cocktails while you check out the scene. 2406 18th St. NW, Adams-Morgan, tel. 202/483–3549. Metro: Woodley Park/Zoo.

HAWK AND DOVE. The regulars at this friendly bar—set in a neighborhood dominated by the Capitol and the Library of Congress—include politicos, lobbyists, and well-behaved marines from a nearby barracks. 329 Pennsylvania Ave. SE, Capitol Hill, tel. 202/543–3300. Metro: Eastern Market.

MADAM'S ORGAN. Neon lights behind the bar and artwork from local artists add to the gritty, urban feel that infuses Madam's Organ. Hill staffers rub shoulders with dreadlocked bike messengers and college students. 2461 18th St. NW, Adams-Morgan, tel. 202/667–5370. Metro: Woodley Park/Zoo.

MIMI'S AMERICAN BISTRO. Swift to become a neighborhood sensation, Mimi's has some of the city's most talented performers, working as "singing servers." Expect to be mesmerized by their renditions of beloved standards, campy torch songs, and fun pop tunes. 2120 P St. NW, Dupont Circle, tel. 202/464–6464. Metro: Dupont Circle.

OZIO RESTAURANT AND LOUNGE. The first floor of this four-story art deco martini and cigar lounge has a humidor and cozy plush couches. Head to the upper floors for dancing and VIP service. Long lines of sharply dressed hipsters stretch in front on weekends. Dig out your Manolo Blahniks—looks count here. 1813 M St. NW, Dupont Circle, tel. 202/822–6000. Metro: Dupont Circle.

TRYST. Ultrahip yet unpretentious, this coffeehouse–bar serves homemade waffles, fancy Italian sandwiches, cocktails, and exotic coffee creations. Comfy chairs and couches fill the big open space, where you can sit for hours. 2459 18th St. NW, Adams-Morgan, tel. 202/232–5500. Metro: Woodley Park/Zoo.

Comedy Clubs

CAPITOL STEPS. The musical political satire of this group of current and former Hill staffers is presented in the high-tech, 600-seat amphitheater of the Ronald Reagan Building and International Trade Center Friday and Saturday at 7:30 PM. Tickets are available through Ticketmaster or from the D.C. Visitor Information Center. Ronald Reagan Building and International Trade Center, 1300 Pennsylvania Ave. NW, tel. 703/683–8330 Capitol Steps, www.capsteps.com. Metro: Federal Triangle.

GROSS NATIONAL PRODUCT. After years of spoofing Republican administrations with such shows as Man Without a Contra, then aiming its barbs at the Democrats in Clintoons and All the President's Women, this satirical comedy troupe was most recently performing Son of a Bush. tel. 202/783–7212, www.gnpcomedy.com.

IMPROV. A heavyweight on the Washington comedy scene, the Improv is descended from the club that sparked the stand-up boomlet in New York City and across the country. Well-known headliners are common. *1140 Connecticut Ave. NW, Downtown, tel. 202/296–7008, www.dcimprov.com. Metro: Farragut North.*

WASHINGTON IMPROV THEATER (WIT). The WIT presents its irreverent humor to sellout crowds at area theaters and clubs. Refreshingly, the troupe's comedy tends not to focus strictly on Beltway politics, and relies heavily on audience suggestions. *Tel. 202/244–8630 for location and reservations, www.dcwit.com.*

Dance Clubs

HABANA VILLAGE. No matter what the temperature outside, it's always balmy inside Habana Village. The tiny dance floor is packed nightly with couples moving to the latest salsa and merengue tunes. When it's time to cool down, you can head to one of several lounges in this converted four-story town house and relax in a wicker chair surrounded by potted palms. Be sure to order a *mojito*, the house special, made of white rum, sugar, and fresh crushed mint leaves. *1834 Columbia Rd. NW, Adams-Morgan, tel. 202/462–6310. Metro: Woodley Park/Zoo.*

PLATINUM. Known for years as the Bank, this upscale dance venue always keeps up with the trends. The DJs play techno, hip-hop, house, and Latin music at the multilevel club, which has three dance floors and a VIP lounge. *915 F St. NW, Downtown, tel. 202/393–3555. Metro: Metro Center.*

POLLY ESTHER'S. Polly Esther's is the Hard Rock Cafe of dance clubs. Current tunes are spun, but '70s and '80s standbys are the crowd-pleasers. Catering to a crowd barely old enough to remember the tail end of the disco era, the club provides an unpretentious good time, especially for groups. Sing out loud to your favorite Bee Gees song while striking a John Travolta pose, and no one will look twice. Tennis shoes and baseball caps, however, do stand out, and are not considered appropriate attire. *605 12th St. NW, Downtown, tel. 202/737–1970. Metro: Metro Center.*

STATE OF THE UNION. A young, eclectic crowd dressed in styles of today's casually hip are the regulars at State. Patrons tend to be serious music fans who come to dance or hold down a spot at the bar while the city's best DJs spin a mix of hip-hop, house, jungle, and R&B. *1357 U St. NW, U Street corridor, tel. 202/588–8926. Metro: U Street/Cardozo.*

Gay and Lesbian Dance Clubs

BADLANDS. One of the best things about Badlands is that it's open on weeknights, when most other clubs are closed. Men will find a definite meat-market vibe here, but with less attitude than at larger nightclubs. *1432 22nd St. NW, Dupont Circle, tel. 202/296–0505. Metro: Dupont Circle.*

CHAOS. You could walk right by this basement-level restaurant/nightclub if it weren't for all the gorgeous guys spilling up the stairs into the street on Fridays and Saturdays. A lesbian crowd takes over on Wednesday, and Thursday is Latin night. *17th and Q Sts. NW, Dupont Circle, tel. 202/232–4141. Metro: Dupont Circle.*

HUNG JURY. You can count on the women at the Hung Jury to make the most of the dance floor, where you're just as likely to hear the innuendo-laden lyrics of rapper Lil' Kim as you are a Top 40 dance track. *1819 H St. NW, Downtown, tel. 202/785–8181. Metro: Farragut West.*

Jazz and Blues Clubs

The **D.C. BLUES SOCIETY HOTLINE** (tel. 202/828–3028, www.dcblues.org) is a clearinghouse for information on upcoming shows, festivals, and jam sessions.

BLUES ALLEY. The restaurant turns out Creole cooking, while cooking on stage you'll find such nationally known performers as Nancy Wilson, Joshua Redman, and Stanley Turrentine. You can come for just the show, but those who come for a meal get better seats. 1073 Wisconsin Ave. NW, rear, Georgetown, tel. 202/337–4141, www.bluesalley.com. Metro: Foggy Bottom.

COLUMBIA STATION. This place is a neighborhood favorite, with good food and great music. The nightly live music usually consists of a quality local jazz band and sometimes blues. Either way, there's usually an electric bass, rather than an upright, to help pound out tunes funky enough for dancing. 2325 18th St. NW, Adams-Morgan, tel. 202/462–6040. Metro: Woodley Park/Zoo.

HR-57 CENTER FOR THE PRESERVATION OF JAZZ AND BLUES. Known locally as HR-57, this isn't really a club or a lounge, but a nonprofit cultural center that spotlights musicians based in the D.C. area, many with national followings. Beer and wine are available. 1610 14th St. NW, Logan Circle, tel. 202/667–3700, www.hr57.org. Metro: U Street/Cardozo.

NEW VEGAS LOUNGE. This sweet dive bar is the home of Dr. Blues, and he doesn't allow any soft-jazz-bluesy-fusion in his house. Even during the weekly open-jam session, it's strictly no-nonsense wailing guitar rhythms by seasoned local players. 1415 P St. NW, Dupont Circle, tel. 202/483–3971. Metro: Dupont Circle.

TWIN'S LOUNGE. This venerable jazz standby is a haven for some of D.C.'s strongest straight-ahead players, as well as for groups from New York City. The club's menu offers tasty Ethiopian appetizers along with staples like nachos, wings, and burgers. 1344 U St. NW, U Street corridor, tel. 202/234–0072. Metro: U Street/Cardozo.

Rock and Pop Clubs

BLACK CAT. This is the place to see the latest local bands as well as a few up-and-coming indie stars from such labels as TeenBeat and Dischord Records. Occasionally, you can see larger acts, like Sleater-Kinney or G. Love. The post-punk crowd whiles away the time in the Red Room, a side bar with pool tables, an eclectic jukebox, and no cover charge. *1831 14th St. NW, U Street corridor, tel. 202/667–7960, www.blackcatdc.com. Metro: U Street/Cardozo.*

NATION. As one of the largest venues for alternative and rock music in Washington (it holds 1,000 people), Nation brings in such acts as 311, Alicia Keys, and Pink. On a separate side of the club, you can gyrate to a mix of mostly alternative dance music. On Friday night this warehouse space becomes "Buzz," a massive rave featuring the latest permutations of techno and drum-and-bass music. *1015 Half St. SE, Southeast, tel. 202/554–1500. Metro: Navy Yard.*

9:30 CLUB. Local, national, and international artists, most of whom fall into the alternative-music category, are booked at this trendy club. You can see the show from a balcony on three sides of the space or from the large dance floor in front of the stage. Vegetarian food catered from Planet X provides nourishment. *815 V St. NW, U Street corridor, tel. 202/393–0930, www.930.com. Metro: U Street/Cardozo.*

VELVET LOUNGE. Squeeze up the narrow stairway and check out the eclectic local and national bands that play at this unassuming little joint. Indie mainstays are regulars, but you'll also find acclaimed up-and-comers. The bar books bands that play psychobilly, alt-country, indie pop . . . you name it, it's here. *915 U St. NW, U Street corridor, tel. 202/462–3213. Metro: U Street/Cardozo.*

THE ARTS

Concert Halls

CRAMTON AUDITORIUM. This 1,500-seat auditorium on the Howard University campus regularly presents jazz, gospel, and R&B concerts. It is also the site of many special events. *2455 6th*

St. NW, Howard University, tel. 202/806–7194. Metro: Shaw–Howard Univ.

DAR CONSTITUTION HALL. Visiting musicians perform everything from jazz to pop to rap at the 3,700-seat Constitution Hall. *18th and C Sts. NW, Downtown, tel. 202/628–4780. Metro: Farragut West.*

JOHN F. KENNEDY CENTER FOR THE PERFORMING ARTS. Any search for cultured entertainment should start here. The "KenCen" is actually five stages under one roof: the Concert Hall, home of the National Symphony Orchestra (NSO); the Eisenhower Theater, usually used for drama; the Terrace Theater, a Philip Johnson–designed space that showcases chamber groups and experimental works; and the Theater Lab, home to cabaret-style performances. You can catch a free performance every evening at 6 PM on the Millennium Stage in the center's Grand Foyer. At this writing, the 2,200-seat Opera House is closed for renovations and is scheduled to reopen in December 2003. In the meantime, Washington Opera plans to hold performances at DAR Constitution Hall. *New Hampshire Ave. and Rock Creek Pkwy. NW, Foggy Bottom, tel. 202/467–4600 or 800/444–1324, www.kennedy-center.org. Metro: Foggy Bottom/GWU (free shuttle-bus service every 15 min on performance days).*

LISNER AUDITORIUM. A 1,500-seat theater on the campus of George Washington University, Lisner Auditorium is the setting for pop, classical, and choral music shows, modern dance performances, and musical theater. *21st and H Sts. NW, Foggy Bottom, tel. 202/994–6800, www.gwu.edu/~lisner. Metro: Foggy Bottom/GWU.*

MCI CENTER. This 19,000-seat arena hosts concerts, ice-skating events, and the circus. Parking can be a problem, but the arena is conveniently situated near several Metro lines. *601 F St. NW, Chinatown, tel. 202/628–3200, www.mcicenter.com. Metro: Gallery Place/Chinatown.*

NATIONAL GALLERY OF ART. Free concerts by the National Gallery Orchestra and performances by visiting classical and jazz ensembles are held in the venerable West Building's West Garden Court on Sunday evening from October to June. Entry is first-come, first-served. *6th St. and Constitution Ave. NW, The Mall, tel. 202/842–6941 or 202/842–6698, www.nga.gov. Metro: Archives/ Navy Memorial.*

SMITHSONIAN INSTITUTION. Jazz, musical theater, and popular standards are performed in the National Museum of American History. In the museum's third-floor Hall of Musical Instruments, musicians periodically play instruments from the museum's collection. The Smithsonian Associates sponsors programs that offer everything from a cappella groups to Cajun zydeco bands; all events require tickets, and locations vary. The annual Smithsonian's Folk Life festival, held on the Mall in June and July, is one of the city's most anticipated events. *1000 Jefferson Dr. SW, The Mall, tel. 202/357–2700; 202/357–2020 recording; 202/357–3030 Smithsonian Associates, www.si.edu. Metro: Smithsonian.*

Dance

DANCE PLACE. A studio theater that presented its first performance in 1980, Dance Place hosts a wide assortment of modern and ethnic dance shows most weekends. It also conducts dance classes daily. *3225 8th St. NE, Catholic University, tel. 202/269–1600, www.danceplace.org. Metro: Brookland/CUA.*

JOY OF MOTION. A dance studio by day, Joy of Motion is the home of several area troupes that perform in the studio's Jack Guidone Theatre by night, including City Dance Ensemble (modern), the Spanish Dance Ensemble (flamenco), and JazzDanz.dc. Two additional studios in Dupont Circle and Bethesda offer classes only. *5207 Wisconsin Ave. NW, Friendship Heights, tel. 202/362–3042, www.joyofmotion.org. Metro: Friendship Heights.*

WASHINGTON BALLET. Between September and May, this company presents classical and contemporary ballets—including works by such choreographers as George Balanchine, Choo-San Goh, and artistic director Septime Webre—at the Kennedy Center and the Warner Theatre. Each December the Washington Ballet performs *The Nutcracker.* tel. 202/362–3606, www.washingtonballet.org.

Film

The international film festival **FILMFEST DC** (Box 21396, 20004, tel. 202/724–5613, www.filmfestdc.org) takes place every year in late April and early May at various venues throughout the city.

AMERICAN FILM INSTITUTE. Filmmakers and actors are often present to discuss their work at this theater showing contemporary and classic foreign and American films. *John F. Kennedy Center for the Performing Arts, New Hampshire Ave. and Rock Creek Pkwy. NW, Foggy Bottom,* tel. 202/785–4600, www.kennedy-center.org. Metro: Foggy Bottom/GWU.

CINEPLEX ODEON UPTOWN. You don't find many like this old beauty anymore: one huge, multiplex-dwarfing screen; art deco flourishes instead of a bland, boxy interior; a wonderful balcony; and—in one happy concession to modernity—crystalline Dolby sound. *3426 Connecticut Ave. NW, Cleveland Park,* tel. 202/966–5400 or 202/966–5401. Metro: Cleveland Park.

HIRSHHORN MUSEUM AND SCULPTURE GARDEN. If you love avant-garde and experimental film, check out the weekly movies—often first-run documentaries, features, and short films—shown here for free. *Independence Ave. and 7th St. SW, The Mall,* tel. 202/357–2700, hirshhorn.si.edu. Metro: Smithsonian or L'Enfant Plaza.

NATIONAL ARCHIVES. Historical films are shown here daily. Call the information line or order a calendar of events for listings. *Constitution Ave. between 7th and 9th Sts. NW, The Mall, tel. 202/501–5000. Metro: Archives/Navy Memorial.*

NATIONAL GALLERY OF ART, EAST BUILDING. Free classic and international films, often complementing exhibits, are shown in this museum's large auditorium. You can pick up a film calendar at the museum. *Constitution Ave., between 3rd and 4th Sts. NW, The Mall, tel. 202/737–4215, www.nga.gov. Metro: Archives/Navy Memorial.*

NATIONAL GEOGRAPHIC SOCIETY. Free educational films with a scientific, geographic, or anthropological focus are shown here weekly. *17th and M Sts. NW, Dupont Circle, tel. 202/857–7588. Metro: Farragut North.*

Music

CHAMBER MUSIC

CORCORAN GALLERY OF ART. Hungary's Takacs String Quartet and the Cleveland Quartet are among the chamber groups that appear in the Corcoran's Musical Evening Series, one Friday each month from October to May (there are also some summer offerings). Concerts are followed by a reception with the artists. *17th St. and New York Ave. NW, Downtown, tel. 202/639–1700, www.corcoran.org. Metro: Farragut West.*

FOLGER SHAKESPEARE LIBRARY. The library's internationally acclaimed resident chamber music ensemble, the Folger Consort, regularly presents a selection of instrumental and vocal pieces from the medieval, Renaissance, and Baroque periods. The season runs from October to May. *201 E. Capitol St. SE, Capitol Hill, tel. 202/544–7077, www.folger.edu. Metro: Union Station or Capitol South.*

NATIONAL ACADEMY OF SCIENCES. The National Musical Arts Chamber Ensemble and the United States Marines Chamber Orchestra perform regularly at free concerts, given fall through spring. The 670-seat auditorium has almost perfect acoustics. *2100 C St. NW, Downtown, tel. 202/334–2436, www.nationalacademies.org. Metro: Foggy Bottom/GWU.*

CHORAL MUSIC
BASILICA OF THE NATIONAL SHRINE OF THE IMMACULATE CONCEPTION. Choral and church groups occasionally perform at the largest Catholic church in the Americas. *400 Michigan Ave. NE, Catholic University, tel. 202/526–8300, www.nationalshrine.com. Metro: Brookland/CUA.*

CHORAL ARTS SOCIETY OF WASHINGTON. The 190-voice Choral Arts Society choir performs a varied selection of classical pieces at the Kennedy Center from September to June. *Tel. 202/244–3669.*

WASHINGTON NATIONAL CATHEDRAL. Choral and church groups frequently perform in this grand cathedral. Admission is usually free. *Massachusetts and Wisconsin Aves. NW, Upper Northwest, tel. 202/537–6207 or 202/537–6247, www.choralarts.org. Metro: Tenleytown/AU.*

OPERA
SUMMER OPERA THEATER COMPANY. An independent professional troupe, the Summer Opera Theater Company stages one opera in June and one in July. *Hartke Theater, Catholic University, Brookland, 620 Michigan Ave. NE, Catholic University, tel. 202/526–1669. Metro: Brookland/CUA.*

WASHINGTON OPERA. Seven operas are performed each season (September–May). Spring 2003 performances are scheduled to be held at DAR Constitution Hall, displaced from the Kennedy Center Opera House while that space undergoes renovations. Performances are often sold out to subscribers, but you can purchase returned tickets an hour before curtain time. Standing-room tickets for the fall season go on sale each Saturday at 10 AM for the following week's performances. At this writing, a new location for ticket sales has not been determined. Call for up-to-date information. *DAR Constitution Hall, 18th and C Sts. NW, Downtown, tel. 202/295–2400 or 800/876–7372, www.dc-opera.org. Metro: Farragut West.*

ORCHESTRA

NATIONAL SYMPHONY ORCHESTRA. The season at the Kennedy Center is from September to June. In summer the NSO performs at Wolf Trap and gives free concerts at the Carter Barron Amphitheatre and, on Memorial Day and Labor Day weekends and July 4, on the West Lawn of the Capitol. The cheapest way to hear the NSO perform in the Kennedy Center Concert Hall is to get $19 second-tier side seats. *Tel. 202/416–8100, www.nationalsymphony.org.*

Theater and Performance Art

COMMERCIAL THEATERS

ARENA STAGE. The city's most-respected resident company (established in 1950), this was also the first outside New York to win a Tony award. It presents a wide-ranging season in its three theaters: the Fichandler Stage, the proscenium Kreeger, and the cabaret-style Old Vat Room. *6th St. and Maine Ave. SW, Waterfront, tel. 202/488–3300, www.arenastage.org. Metro: Waterfront.*

FORD'S THEATRE. Looking much as it did when President Lincoln was shot at a performance of *Our American Cousin*, Ford's hosts both dramas and musicals, many with family appeal. Dickens's *A Christmas Carol* is presented every year. *511 10th St. NW, Downtown, tel. 202/347–4833, www.fordstheatre.org. Metro: Metro Center.*

LINCOLN THEATRE. From the 1920s to the 1940s, the Lincoln hosted the same performers as the Cotton Club and the Apollo Theatre in New York City: Cab Calloway, Lena Horne, Duke Ellington. Today the 1,250-seater shows films and welcomes such acts as the Count Basie Orchestra and the Harlem Boys and

Girls Choir. *1215 U St. NW, U Street corridor, tel. 202/328–6000. Metro: U St./Cardozo.*

NATIONAL THEATRE. In the same location since 1835, the National Theatre presents touring Broadway shows. From September through April, look for free children's shows on Saturday, and free Monday night shows that could be anything from Asian dance to a cappella cabarets. *1321 Pennsylvania Ave. NW, Downtown, tel. 202/628–6161, www.nationaltheatre.org. Metro: Metro Center.*

SHAKESPEARE THEATRE. Five plays—three by the Bard and two classics from his era—are staged each year by the acclaimed Shakespeare Theatre troupe in a state-of-the-art, 450-seat space. For two weeks each June the company offers a free play under the stars at Carter Barron Amphitheatre. *450 7th St. NW, Downtown, tel. 202/547–1122, www.shakespearedc.org. Metro: Gallery Place/Chinatown or Archives/Navy Memorial.*

WARNER THEATRE. One of Washington's grand theaters, this 1924 building hosts road shows, dance recitals, pop music, and the occasional comedy act. *1299 Pennsylvania Ave. NW, Downtown, tel. 202/783–4000. Metro: Metro Center.*

SMALL THEATERS AND COMPANIES

DISTRICT OF COLUMBIA ARTS CENTER. Known by area artists as DCAC, this cross-genre space shows changing exhibits in its gallery and presents avant-garde performance art and experimental plays in its small black-box theater. *2438 18th St. NW, Adams-Morgan, tel. 202/462–7833, www.dcartscenter.org. Metro: Woodley Park/Zoo.*

FOLGER SHAKESPEARE LIBRARY. Look for three to four productions a year of Shakespeare or Shakespeare-influenced works, all staged in the library's little jewel box of a theater. With room for 250, the theater is a replica of the in-yard theaters popular in Shakespeare's time. *201 E. Capitol St. SE, Capitol Hill,* tel. 202/544–4600, *www.folger.edu*. Metro: Union Station or Capitol South.

SOURCE THEATRE. Established plays with a sharp satirical edge and modern interpretations of classics are presented at this 125-seat theater. Every July and August, Source hosts the Washington Theater Festival, a series of new plays, many by local playwrights. *1835 14th St. NW, U Street corridor, tel. 202/462–1073, users.starpower.net/sourcetheatre*. Metro: U Street/Cardozo.

STUDIO THEATRE. One of the busiest groups in the city, this small independent company has an eclectic season of classic and offbeat plays. Two 200-seat theaters—the Mead and the Milton—as well as the 50-seat Secondstage (home to experimental works) are contained in the spacious building. *1333 P St. NW, Dupont Circle, tel. 202/332–3300, www.studiotheatre.org*. Metro: Dupont Circle.

WOOLLY MAMMOTH. Unusual, imaginatively produced shows have earned Woolly Mammoth good reviews and favorable comparisons to Chicago's Steppenwolf. At this writing, the company is temporarily sharing space at the Kennedy Center's American Film Institute (AFI) Theater. *tel. 202/393–3939, www.woollymammoth.net*.

In This Chapter

Updated by Robin Dougherty

where to stay

WITH MORE THAN 340 LOCATIONS offering upward of 63,000 guest rooms in the D.C. area, you can almost always find a place to stay—though it's prudent to make reservations. Hotels are often full of conventioneers, politicians in transit, or families, and, in spring, school groups. Rates are especially high around the Cherry Blossom Festival in April. Graduation and other big college weekends at Georgetown and George Washington University also strain the system. Rates drop in late December and January, except around an inauguration.

Hotels' parking fees range from free to $24 (plus tax) per night. This sometimes involves valet parking. Street parking is free on Sunday and usually after 6:30 PM. But there are often far more cars searching than there are spaces available. During weekday rush hours many streets are unavailable for parking; illegally parked cars are towed, and reclaiming a car is expensive and very inconvenient.

For a list of its member hotels, contact the **WASHINGTON, D.C., CONVENTION TOURISM CORP.** (1212 New York Ave. NW, Downtown 20005, tel. 202/789–7000). To find reasonably priced accommodations in small guest houses and private homes, try **BED 'N' BREAKFAST ACCOMMODATIONS LTD. OF WASHINGTON, D.C.** (Box 12011, 20005, tel. 202/328–3510, www.bedandbreakfastdc.com), which is staffed weekdays 10–5. It handles about 85 different properties in the area. The **BED AND BREAKFAST LEAGUE, LTD.** (Box 9490, 20016, tel. 202/362–7767) can send you a list of its properties with accommodations priced to please.

The lodgings we list are the cream of the crop in each price category. We always list the facilities that are available—but we don't specify whether they cost extra: when pricing accommodations, always ask what's included and what costs extra. All hotels listed have private bath unless otherwise noted.

CATEGORY	COST*
$$$$	over $270
$$$	$205–$270
$$	$145–$205
$	under $145

*All prices are for a standard double room, excluding room tax (14.5%). A $3.44 per night energy charge is also applied to the total.

Assume that hotels operate on the **EUROPEAN PLAN** (EP, with no meals) unless we specify that they use the **CONTINENTAL PLAN** (CP, with a Continental breakfast), **BREAKFAST PLAN** (BP, with a full cooked breakfast), **MODIFIED AMERICAN PLAN** (MAP, with breakfast and dinner), or the **FULL AMERICAN PLAN** (FAP, with all meals).

CAPITOL HILL

$$$ **HOTEL GEORGE.** A hip standout amid Washington's more sedate
★ lodgings, this contemporary hotel has bright and airy guest rooms, with granite-topped work desks and marble bathrooms. Portraits of America's first president, created by Andy Warhol protégé Steve Kaufman, adorn rooms and public areas. Business travelers are well provided for, with ample work space, high-speed modem access, and a 24-hour fitness center. At this small hotel, the staff not only recognizes you, they give you personal attention. Bistro Bis, one of the city's finest restaurants, serves updated classic French dishes. 15 E St. NW, Capitol Hill 20001, tel. 202/347-4200 or 800/576-8331, fax 202/347-4213, www. hotelgeorge.com. 139 rooms. Restaurant, room service, in-room data ports, minibars, cable TV, in-room VCRs, gym, steam rooms, billiards, bar,

lobby lounge, meeting rooms, parking (fee). AE, D, DC, MC, V. Metro: Union Station.

$$$ **WASHINGTON COURT HOTEL.** Terraced marble stairs lead to an atrium lobby with a skylight, indoor waterfall, and glass elevators at this hotel with wonderful views of the Capitol. The discerning eye may appreciate the inlaid wood and stained glass—two of the hotel's original art deco elements. Guest rooms are spacious and equipped with modern, luxurious furnishings and high-speed modem access. 525 New Jersey Ave. NW, Capitol Hill 20001, tel. 202/ 628–2100, fax 202/879–7918. 252 rooms, 12 suites. Restaurant, room service, in-room data ports, refrigerators, cable TV, health club, bar, dry cleaning, laundry service, business services, parking (fee). AE, D, DC, MC, V. Metro: Union Station.

$$–$$$ **CAPITOL HILL SUITES.** On a quiet residential street beside the Library of Congress, this all-suites hotel's proximity to the U.S. House of Representatives office buildings means that it's often filled with visiting lobbyists when Congress is in session. Guest rooms, which are actually renovated apartments, are large and cozy; the sun-filled lobby has a fireplace. 200 C St. SE, Capitol Hill 20003, tel. 202/543–6000, 800/424–9165, or 888/627–7811, fax 202/547–2608. 152 suites. In-room data ports, kitchenettes, refrigerators, cable TV, gym, health club, lobby lounge, dry cleaning, laundry service, business services, meeting rooms, parking (fee). AE, D, DC, MC, V. CP. Metro: Capitol South.

DOWNTOWN

$$$$ **HAY-ADAMS HOTEL.** Two famous Americans—statesman and
★ author John Hay and diplomat and historian Henry Adams— once owned homes on the site where this Italian Renaissance– style landmark structure now stands. The hotel is both contemporary and elegant; many rooms have fireplaces and a view of the White House. An attentive staff assures congenial service. The Lafayette Room restaurant serves elegant contemporary American cuisine. 1 Lafayette Sq. NW, Downtown 20006, tel. 202/638–

washington lodging

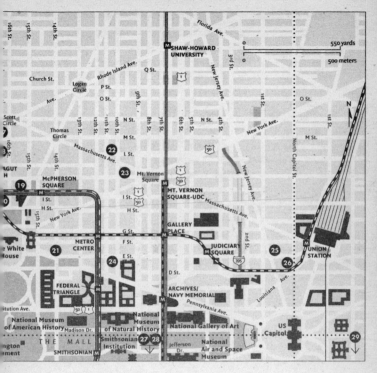

Washington
Court Hotel, 25

Westin
Fairfax Hotel, 9

Willard Inter-
Continental, 21

6600, 800/424–5054, or 800/853–6807, fax 202/638–2716 or 202/638–3803, www.hayadams.com. 125 rooms, 20 suites. Restaurant, room service, in-room data ports, minibars, some refrigerators, cable TV, bar, dry cleaning, laundry service, business services, airport shuttle, parking (fee), some pets allowed. AE, D, DC, MC, V. Metro: McPherson Square or Farragut North.

$$$$ JEFFERSON HOTEL. Federal-style elegance abounds at this small
★ luxury hotel. American antiques and original art fill each room, which all have CD players. There's a high staff-to-guest ratio and service is outstanding—employees greet you by name and laundry is hand-ironed and delivered in wicker baskets. The Dining Room restaurant, which serves American cuisine, is a favorite of high-ranking politicos and visiting film stars. 1200 16th St. NW, Downtown 20036, tel. 202/347–2200 or 800/368–5966, fax 202/331–8474, www.loewshotels.com. 68 rooms, 32 suites. Restaurant, room service, in-room data ports, some microwaves, cable TV, in-room VCRs, bar, laundry service, business services, parking (fee). AE, D, DC, MC, V. Metro: Farragut North.

$$$$ WILLARD INTER-CONTINENTAL. If you expect nothing short of
★ perfection, you might try this longtime favorite of American presidents and other news-makers. Martin Luther King Jr. drafted his "I Have a Dream" speech here. Superb service and a wealth of amenities are hallmarks of the hotel. The spectacular beaux arts main lobby has columns, sparkling chandeliers, mosaic floors, and elaborate ceilings. Rooms have elegant yet comfortable turn-of-the-20th-century reproduction furniture and sleek marble bathrooms. Some rooms have views of the Capitol building or the Washington Monument. The formal dining room, the Willard Room, has won nationwide acclaim. 1401 Pennsylvania Ave. NW, Downtown 20004, tel. 202/628–9100, fax 202/637–7326, www.washington.interconti.com. 299 rooms, 42 suites. Restaurant, café, room service, in-room data ports, in-room safes, minibars, some microwaves, cable TV, health club, 2 bars, dry cleaning, laundry service, business services, meeting rooms, parking (fee), some pets allowed. AE, D, DC, MC, V. Metro: Metro Center.

$$$-$$$$ HENLEY PARK HOTEL. Built in 1918, this Tudor-style building adorned with over 100 gargoyles has the cozy charm of an English country house. The highly acclaimed Coeur de Lion restaurant has a leafy atrium, stained-glass windows, and an American menu. The hotel lobby is warm and inviting, with a fireplace and grandfather clock. Rooms are decorated with Edwardian-style furnishings but have modern amenities. Shoe shines, morning delivery of the *Washington Post*, and afternoon tea are a few of the perks here. *926 Massachusetts Ave. NW, Downtown 20001, tel. 202/ 638–5200 or 800/222–8474, fax 202/638–6740, www.henleypark.com. 96 rooms, 17 suites. Restaurant, room service, in-room data ports, in-room safes, minibars, refrigerators, cable TV, bar, business services, parking (fee), some pets allowed. AE, D, DC, MC, V. Metro: Metro Center or Gallery Place/Chinatown.*

$$$-$$$$ MORRISON-CLARK INN. The elegant merger of two 1864 Victorian
★ town houses, this inn functioned as the Soldiers, Sailors, Marines and Airmen's Club in the early 1900s. The antiques-filled public rooms have marble fireplaces, bay windows, 14-ft pier mirrors, and porch access, and one house has a 1917 Chinese Chippendale porch. Rooms have neoclassic, French country, or Victorian furnishings. American cuisine with southern and other regional influences is served at the inn's highly regarded restaurant, which has a popular brunch. *1015 L St. NW, Downtown 20001, tel. 202/898– 1200 or 800/332–7898, fax 202/289–8576. 42 rooms, 12 suites. Restaurant, room service, in-room data ports, minibars, cable TV, in-room VCRs, gym, dry cleaning, laundry service, business services, parking (fee). AE, D, DC, MC, V. CP. Metro: Metro Center.*

$$-$$$$ ST. REGIS. With gilded ornamental ceilings and Louis XVI furnishings, this luxurious hotel in a bustling business sector near the White House resembles an updated Italian Renaissance mansion. Service is unpretentious but attentive, and the top floor has day and night butler service. Cordless phones, Frette sheets, and Bose radios are found in every room. Children stay free in their parents' room. The Lespinasse restaurant, with renowned French cuisine, is cousin to the New York original. The outdoor pool is heated. *923 16th St. NW, Downtown 20006, tel. 202/638–2626 or 800/ 325–3535, fax 202/638–4231. 180 rooms, 14 suites. Restaurant, room service, in-room data ports, in-room safes, minibars, refrigerators, cable TV, pool, gym, bar, lobby lounge, baby-sitting, business services, meeting rooms, parking (fee), some pets allowed. AE, D, DC, MC, V. Metro: McPherson Square.*

$$–$$$ **HOTEL WASHINGTON.** Since opening in 1918, the Hotel Washington has been known for its view. Washingtonians bring out-of-towners to the open-air rooftop bar (May–October) for a panorama that includes the White House grounds and the Washington Monument. Now a National Landmark, the hotel sprang from the drawing boards of John Carrère and Thomas Hastings, who designed the New York Public Library. Guest rooms have 18th-century mahogany reproductions and Italian marble bathrooms. Rooms in the interior portion of the hotel are small. *515 15th St. NW, Downtown 20004, tel. 202/638–5900, fax 202/638– 4275, www.hotelwashington.com. 344 rooms, 16 suites. 2 restaurants, snack bar, room service, in-room data ports, cable TV, gym, hair salon, sauna, bar, lobby lounge, dry cleaning, laundry service, business services, parking (fee), some pets allowed. AE, D, DC, MC, V. Metro: Metro Center.*

$ **HOTEL HARRINGTON.** One of Washington's oldest continuously operating hotels, the Harrington doesn't offer many frills, but it does have low prices and a location right at the center of everything. *436 11th St. NW, Downtown 20004, tel. 202/628–8140 or 800/424– 8532, fax 202/347–3924, www.hotelharrington.com. 246 rooms, 36 suites. Restaurant, cafeteria, room service, cable TV, hair salon, bar, pub, laundry facilities, business services, meeting rooms, parking (fee), some pets allowed. AE, D, DC, MC, V. Metro: Metro Center.*

DUPONT CIRCLE

$$$–$$$$ **CHURCHILL HOTEL.** This newly renovated property, right outside ★ Dupont Circle, offers comfort and elegance. All rooms have a small work area, and the building's excellent hilltop location

means that many guest rooms have excellent views of Washington. The staff goes out of its way to be helpful, and children under 12 stay for free. The Chart Grill serves three meals daily. *1914 Connecticut Ave. NW, Dupont Circle 20009, tel. 202/797–2000 or 800/424–2464, fax 202/462–0944. 107 rooms, 37 suites. Restaurant, room service, in-room safes, in-room data ports, minibars, cable TV, gym, bar, dry cleaning, laundry service, business services, parking (fee), some pets allowed (fee). AE, D, DC, MC, V. Metro: Dupont Circle.*

$$$–$$$$ **WESTIN FAIRFAX HOTEL.** The Gore family once owned this 1924 former apartment building, which was Al's childhood home. Now an intimate hotel, the Fairfax has an English hunt-club theme and complimentary butler service, and is close to Dupont Circle, Georgetown, and the Kennedy Center. Rooms have views of Embassy Row or Georgetown and the National Cathedral. The renowned Jockey Club restaurant, with its half-timber ceilings, dark-wood paneling, and red-checker tablecloths, serves three meals daily. The Fairfax Bar is a cozy spot for a drink beside the fire, with piano entertainment some evenings. *2100 Massachusetts Ave. NW, Dupont Circle 20008, tel. 202/293–2100 or 800/325–3589, fax 202/293–0641. 154 rooms, 59 suites. Restaurant, room service, in-room data ports, in-room safes, minibars, cable TV, in-room VCRs, gym, massage, sauna, bar, business services, meeting rooms, parking (fee). AE, D, DC, MC, V. Metro: Dupont Circle.*

$$–$$$ **ROUGE HOTEL.** This hotel strives and succeeds at bringing
★ Florida's South Beach club scene to D.C. Guest rooms are decorated with swank eye-catching furniture that make them seem like an extension of the hip lobby lounge, where the bartenders are busy concocting sweet new drinks. Bar Rouge, the cocktail lounge, attracts club-going denizens at all hours and serves food nearly around the clock. *1315 16th St. NW, Dupont Circle 20036, tel. 202/232–8000 or 800/368–5689, fax 202/667–9827, www.rougehotel.com. 135 rooms. Restaurant, café, room service, in-room data ports, in-room safes, some kitchenettes, minibars, some refrigerators, some cable TVs with video games, indoor pool, health club,*

hair salon, hot tub, massage, sauna, steam room, racquetball, squash, bar, lobby lounge, business services, parking (fee), some pets allowed. AE, D, DC, MC, V. Metro: Dupont Circle.

$$–$$$ TOPAZ HOTEL. Before they made their respective moves to the White House, both Theodore and Franklin Roosevelt lived at this site—when it was an apartment building. Though the area is sedate, the reputation of the hotel itself is anything but. Its New Age theme is expressed through colorful decor, daily horoscopes, and "power shakes" served in the morning. The popular Topaz Bar draws people from all over town. Rooms have queen-, double queen–, or king-size beds. The rates include admission to the National Health Center. *1733 N St. NW, Dupont Circle 20036, tel. 202/ 393–3000 or 800/424–2950, fax 202/785–9581, www.topazhotel.com. 99 rooms. Restaurant, in-room data ports, in-room safes, kitchenettes, minibars, refrigerators, cable TV, bar, dry cleaning, laundry service, business services, meeting rooms, parking (fee), some pets allowed. AE, D, DC, MC, V. CP. Metro: Dupont Circle.*

$–$$ HOTEL TABARD INN. Three Victorian town houses were consolidated to form the Tabard, one of the oldest hotels in D.C. Although the wooden floorboards are creaky, the hotel exudes a quaint charm and well-worn Victorian and American Empire pieces fill the interior. Room size and facilities vary considerably, as do the prices. Passes are provided to the nearby YMCA, which has extensive fitness facilities. The contemporary restaurant has a cozy courtyard. *1739 N St. NW, Downtown 20036, tel. 202/785– 1277, fax 202/785–6173, www.tabardinn.com. 40 rooms, 25 with bath. Restaurant, in-room data ports, bar, lobby lounge, laundry facilities, business services, parking (fee), some pets allowed; no TV in some rooms. AE, D, DC, MC, V. CP. Metro: Dupont Circle.*

$ ADAM'S INN. Think cozy and rustic and you've captured the essence of this European-style bed-and-breakfast. Spread throughout three residential town houses, the inn has Victorian-style rooms that are small but comfortable. Many rooms share baths, but those that do have a sink in the room. A shared kitchen and limited garage parking are available. There are pay phones in the lobby, and the reception staff takes messages. *1744 Lanier Pl. NW, Woodley Park 20009, tel. 202/745–3600 or 800/578–6807, fax 202/319–7958, www.adamsinn.com. 25 rooms, 15 with bath. Laundry facilities, laundry service, business services, parking (fee); no room phones, no room TVs. AE, D, DC, MC, V. CP. Metro: Woodley Park/Zoo.*

GEORGETOWN

$$$$ FOUR SEASONS HOTEL. Impeccable service and a wealth of
★ amenities have made this a perennial favorite with celebrities, hotel connoisseurs, and families. The hotel overlooks the C&O Canal and Rock Creek. Rich mahogany paneling, antiques, spectacular flower arrangements, and extensive greenery abound. Rooms are spacious and bright, with fine marble baths (some with sunken tubs). CD players and PCs are available for in-room use. The Garden Terrace restaurant has live music six days a week and serves a popular Sunday brunch and daily afternoon tea. *2800 Pennsylvania Ave. NW, Georgetown 20007, tel. 202/342–0444 or 800/332–3442, fax 202/342–1673. 200 rooms, 60 suites. 2 restaurants, room service, in-room data ports, in-room safes, minibars, cable TV, pool, health club, hair salon, sauna, spa, bar, lobby lounge, nightclub, children's programs, concierge, business services, parking (fee), some pets allowed. AE, D, DC, MC, V. Metro: Foggy Bottom.*

$$–$$$$ GEORGETOWN INN. Reminiscent of a gentleman's sporting club, this quiet, federal-era, redbrick hotel seems like something from the 1700s. Guest rooms are large and decorated in a colonial style. The hotel is in the heart of historic Georgetown, near shopping, dining, galleries, and theaters. Free passes to a nearby fitness center are provided. The Daily Grill restaurant serves American cuisine. *1310 Wisconsin Ave. NW, Georgetown 20007, tel. 202/333–8900 or 800/424–2979, fax 202/625–1744, www.georgetowninn.com. 86 rooms, 10 suites. Restaurant, room service, in-room data ports, cable TV, gym, bar, business services, parking (fee). AE, D, DC, MC, V. Metro: Foggy Bottom.*

$$–$$$$ **GEORGETOWN SUITES.** If you consider standard hotel rooms cramped and overpriced, you'll find this establishment a welcome surprise. Consisting of two buildings a block apart in the heart of Georgetown, the hotel has suites of varying sizes. All have large kitchens with dishwashers and separate sitting rooms. *1111 30th St. NW, Georgetown 20007, tel. 202/298–7800 or 800/348–7203, fax 202/333–5792, www.georgetownsuites.com. 216 suites. In-room data ports, kitchenettes, microwaves, gym, dry cleaning, laundry facilities, laundry service, parking (fee). AE, D, DC, MC, V. CP. Metro: Foggy Bottom.*

$$–$$$$ **LATHAM HOTEL.** Many of the immaculate, beautifully decorated rooms at this small European-style hotel on the area's fashionable main avenue have treetop views of the Potomac River and the C&O Canal. The hotel is a favorite of diplomats. The polished brass and glass lobby leads to Citronelle, one of the city's best French restaurants. There's a La Madeleine coffee shop on-site. *3000 M St. NW, Foggy Bottom 20007, tel. 202/726–5000 or 800/368–5922; 800/528–4261 in D.C.; 800/368–5922, fax 202/337–4250, www.thelatham.com. 122 rooms, 21 suites. Restaurant, coffee shop, room service, in-room data ports, cable TV, pool, bar, business services, parking (fee). AE, D, DC, MC, V. Metro: Foggy Bottom.*

SOUTHWEST

$–$$$$ **LOEWS L'ENFANT PLAZA.** An oasis of calm above a Metro stop and a shopping mall, this comfortably furnished hotel has spectacular views of the river, the Capitol, and monuments. The staff is well-trained and efficient. Business travelers in particular take advantage of proximity to government agencies (USDA, USPS, USIA, and DOT). Both bathrooms and bedrooms have TVs and phones. *480 L'Enfant Plaza SW, Downtown 20024, tel. 202/484–1000 or 800/223–0888, fax 202/646–4456. 348 rooms, 22 suites. Restaurant, room service, in-room data ports, minibars, refrigerators, cable TV, in-room VCRs, indoor pool, health club, 2 bars, business services, parking (fee), some pets allowed. AE, D, DC, MC, V. Metro: L'Enfant Plaza.*

$–$$ **CHANNEL INN.** The only hotel on Washington's waterfront, this property overlooks the Washington Channel, the marina, and the Potomac River. All rooms have a small balcony and are decorated with either Laura Ashley or similar-style fabrics. Public areas and meeting rooms are given a nautical motif through mahogany panels and marine artifacts. The terrace allows scenic cocktail quaffing and dining in warm weather. Access to a local health club is free. *650 Water St. SW, Downtown 20024, tel. 202/554–2400 or 800/368–5668, fax 202/863–1164, www.channelinn.com. 100 rooms, 4 suites. Restaurant, café, room service, in-room data ports, cable TV, pool, bar, meeting rooms, free parking. AE, D, DC, MC, V. Metro: Waterfront.*

NORTHWEST/UPPER CONNECTICUT AVENUE

$$$$ **OMNI SHOREHAM HOTEL.** An immense facility with seven ballrooms, this hotel has hosted the world's rich and famous since 1930, when its art deco– and Renaissance–style lobby opened for business. It's still a busy place, with black-tie political events in its famed Regency ballroom many nights of the week. Rooms have cherry-wood furniture and marble-floor baths with phones. *2500 Calvert St. NW, Woodley Park 20008, tel. 202/234–0700 or 800/843–6664, fax 202/756–5145. 836 rooms, 24 suites. Restaurant, snack bar, room service, in-room data ports, minibars, cable TV, pool, health club, bar, shops, dry cleaning, laundry service, business services, parking (fee), some pets allowed. AE, D, DC, MC, V. Metro: Woodley Park/Zoo.*

$–$$ **JURYS NORMANDY INN.** On a quiet street in the embassy area
★ of Connecticut Avenue stands this small, quaint European-style hotel. The cozy rooms come with coffeemakers and are attractively decorated with colonial reproduction furniture. Each Tuesday evening a wine-and-cheese reception is held for guests. Complimentary coffee and tea are available in the morning and afternoon. *2118 Wyoming Ave. NW, Adams-Morgan 20008, tel. 202/483–1350, 800/424–3729, or 800/842–3729, fax 202/387–8241, www.jurysdoyle.com. 75 rooms. Café, in-room data ports, in-room safes,*

refrigerators, cable TV, library, laundry facilities, parking (fee). AE, D, DC, MC, V. CP. Metro: Dupont Circle.

WEST END/FOGGY BOTTOM

$$$$ **MONARCH HOTEL.** Contemporary and traditional meet at this
★ stylish hotel at the Georgetown end of downtown Washington. The glassed lobby and about a third of the bright, airy rooms overlook the central courtyard and gardens—a popular spot for weddings. The informal Bistro restaurant serves contemporary American cuisine and has courtyard dining. The Colonnade room hosts a Sunday champagne brunch. The fitness center is one of the best in the city. 2401 M St. NW, Georgetown 20037, tel. 202/429–2400 or 877/222–2266, fax 202/457–5010, www.monarchdc.com. 406 rooms, 9 suites. Restaurant, café, room service, in-room data ports, in-room safes, minibars, some refrigerators, cable TV, indoor pool, health club, hair salon, hot tub, massage, sauna, steam room, racquetball, squash, bar, lobby lounge, business services, parking (fee), some pets allowed. AE, D, DC, MC, V. Metro: Foggy Bottom/GWU.

$$$$ **PARK HYATT.** Original artwork, some by Picasso, Matisse, and Calder, grace the guest rooms and public spaces of this elegant and luxurious modern hotel, about four blocks from the eastern end of Georgetown, just off M Street. Rooms have built-in armoires, goose-down duvets, and specially commissioned artwork. The Melrose restaurant, which specializes in seafood, has courtyard dining beside a cascading fountain. 1201 24th St. NW, Foggy Bottom 20037, tel. 202/789–1234 or 800/228–9000, fax 202/457–8823. 93 rooms, 131 suites. Restaurant, café, room service, in-room data ports, refrigerators, cable TV, pool, health club, hair salon, hot tub, massage, sauna, spa, steam room, bar (with entertainment), lobby lounge, business services, parking (fee). AE, D, DC, MC, V. Metro: Foggy Bottom/GWU.

$$–$$$$ **ONE WASHINGTON CIRCLE HOTEL.** The combination of elegant rooms and facilities and a coveted location makes this hotel a relative bargain. All accommodations are suites that feel like well-furnished apartments, with separate bedrooms, living rooms, dining areas, balconies, and some full kitchens. The American-style West End Cafe is popular with locals who come for the food and the live music. *1 Washington Circle NW, Foggy Bottom 20037, tel. 202/872–1680 or 800/424–9671, fax 202/223–3961, www.onewashcirclehotel.com. 151 suites. Restaurant, room service, in-room data ports, some kitchens, minibars, refrigerators, cable TV, pool, gym, hair salon, bar, piano, dry cleaning, laundry facilities, laundry service, business services, meeting rooms, parking (fee). AE, D, DC, MC, V. Metro: Foggy Bottom/GWU.*

$$–$$$$ **SWISSÔTEL WASHINGTON WATERGATE.** ★ First Lady Laura Bush chose the tony restaurant of this famed hotel as the site of her first official dinner party in 2001. Soon after, the restaurant became Jeffrey's, which serves sophisticated Southwestern cuisine. The hotel is on the Potomac River, across from the Kennedy Center. Originally intended as apartments, the guest rooms are large, and all have walk-in closets and fax machines. There's complimentary limousine service weekday mornings. *2650 Virginia Ave. NW, Downtown 20037, tel. 202/965–2300 or 800/424–2736, fax 202/ 337–7915. 104 rooms, 146 suites. Restaurant, room service, some kitchens, in-room data ports, in-room safes, minibars, refrigerators, cable TV, indoor pool, health club, hair salon, hot tub, massage, bar, business services, parking (fee), some pets allowed. AE, D, DC, MC, V. Metro: Foggy Bottom/GWU.*

practical information

Air Travel

CARRIERS

All major airlines fly into BWI, Ronald Reagan National, and
Dulles airports, except America West, which doesn't fly into
Dulles. Of the smaller airlines, Air Tran flies to Dulles and
Midwest Express flies to both. Southwest has service to BWI.

➤**MAJOR AIRLINES: Air Canada** (tel. 888/422–7533, www.
aircanada.ca). **America West** (tel. 800/235–9292, www.
americawest.com). **American** (tel. 800/433–7300, www.aa.
com). **Continental** (tel. 800/525–0280, www.continental.com).
Delta (tel. 800/221–1212, www.delta.com). **Northwest** (tel. 800/
225–2525, www.nwa.com). **United** (tel. 800/241–6522, www.
united.com). **US Airways** (tel. 800/428–4322, www.usairways.com).

➤**SMALLER AIRLINES: Air Tran** (tel. 800/825–8538, www.airtran.
com). **Midwest Express** (tel. 800/452–2022, www.midwestexpress.
com). **Southwest** (tel. 800/435–9792, www.southwest.com).

Airports and Transfers

The major gateways to D.C. include Ronald Reagan National
Airport, in Virginia, 4 mi south of downtown Washington; Dulles
International Airport, 26 mi west of Washington; and Baltimore-
Washington International (BWI) Airport, in Maryland, about 30
mi northeast of Washington.

➤AIRPORT INFORMATION: **Baltimore-Washington International Airport** (BWI; tel. 410/859–7100, www.bwiairport.com). **Dulles International Airport** (IAD; tel. 703/572–2700, www.mwaa.com). **Ronald Reagan National Airport** (DCA; tel. 703/417–8000, www.mwaa.com).

TRANSFERS BY BUS

The **Washington Flyer** Coach Service provides a convenient link between Dulles Airport and the West Falls Church (VA) Metro station. The 20-minute ride is $8 one-way or $14 round-trip; buses run every half hour. All coaches are disabled-accessible. Fares may be paid in cash or with Visa or MasterCard; children under age six ride free.

The Washington Metropolitan Area Transit Authority operates an express Metro bus service between downtown Washington, D.C., to Dulles.

Reagan National, Dulles, and BWI airports are served by **SuperShuttle,** which will take you to a specific hotel or residence. Make reservations at the ground transportation desk. Fares vary depending on the destination. The 20-minute ride from Reagan National to downtown averages $9–$13; the 45-minute ride from Dulles runs $22–$25; the 65-minute ride from BWI averages $28–$30; drivers accept major credit cards in addition to cash. The length of the ride varies depending on traffic and the number of stops that need to be made.

➤BUS INFORMATION: **SuperShuttle** (tel. 800/258–3826 or 202/296–6662, www.supershuttle.com). **Washington Flyer** (tel. 888/washfly or 703/572–8400, www.washfly.com). **Washington Metropolitan Area Transit Authority** (WMATA: tel. 202/637–7000; 202/638–3780 TDD, www.metroopensdoors.com).

TRANSFERS BY LIMOUSINE

Private Car has two counters at BWI Airport and charges approximately $70 plus a 15% tip for up to four passengers traveling from there to downtown; or call ahead to have a car waiting for you at Reagan National (approximately $45 plus 15% tip) or Dulles (approximately $85 plus 15% tip). Reservations are a good idea.

➤LIMOUSINE INFORMATION: Private Car (tel. 800/685-0888, www.cinecola.com).

TRANSFERS BY METRO

If you're coming into Ronald Reagan National Airport, have little to carry, and are staying at a hotel near a subway stop, it makes sense to take the Metro. The station is within walking distance of the baggage claim area, but a free airport shuttle bus runs between the Metro station and Terminal A. The Metro ride downtown takes about 20 minutes and costs $1.10–$2, depending on the time of day and your end destination.

TRANSFERS BY TAXI

Expect to pay about $14 to get from Ronald Reagan National Airport to downtown, $50–$65 from Dulles, and $58–$65 from BWI. Unscrupulous cabbies prey on out-of-towners, so if the fare strikes you as astronomical, get the driver's name and cab number and threaten to call the D.C. Taxicab Commission. A $1.50 airport surcharge is added to the total at all airports. A $1 surcharge is added to the total for travel during rush hour.

➤TAXI INFORMATION: D.C. Taxicab Commission (tel. 202/645-6018).

TRANSFERS BY TRAIN

Free shuttle buses carry passengers between airline terminals and the train station at BWI Airport. Amtrak and Maryland Rail Commuter Service (MARC) trains run between BWI and Washington's Union Station from around 6 AM to 10 PM. The cost of the 30-minute ride is $20–$32 on an Amtrak train and $5 on a MARC train, which only runs on weekdays.

►TRAIN INFORMATION: Amtrak (tel. 800/872–7245, www. amtrak.com). Maryland Rail Commuter Service (MARC; tel. 800/325–7245, www.mtamaryland.com).

Bus Travel to and from Washington, D.C.

Washington is a major terminal for Greyhound Bus Lines.

►BUS INFORMATION: Greyhound Bus Lines (1005 1st St. NE, tel. 202/289–5160 or 800/231–2222, www.greyhound.com).

Bus Travel within Washington, D.C.

The red, white, and blue Washington Metropolitan Area Transit Authority (WMATA) Metrobuses crisscross the city and nearby suburbs. Free bus-to-bus transfers, good for two hours, are available on buses. In Metro stations rail-to-bus transfers must be picked up before boarding the train. There is a transfer charge (25¢ on regular Metrobus routes and $1.15 on express routes) when boarding the bus. Transfers are free for senior citizens. There are no bus-to-rail transfers.

FARES AND SCHEDULES

All bus rides within the District are $1.10. All-day passes are available on the bus for $2.50. Complete bus and Metro maps for the metropolitan D.C. area, which note museums, monuments, theaters, and parks, can be purchased for $1.50 at Metro Center or map stores. Call the WMATA for schedule and route information. It's open weekdays 6 AM to 10:30 PM, and weekends 8 AM to 10:30 PM.

►BUS INFORMATION: Washington Metropolitan Area Transit Authority (WMATA; tel. 202/637–7000; 202/638–3780 TDD, www.metroopensdoors.com).

Car Rental

Rates in Washington, D.C., begin at $37 a day and $131 a week for an economy car with air-conditioning, an automatic transmission, and unlimited mileage. This does not include tax on car rentals, which is 8%–11.5% depending on the place from which you're renting, or any airport facility fees.

➤**MAJOR AGENCIES: Alamo** (tel. 800/327–9633; www.alamo. com). **Avis** (tel. 800/331–1212; 800/879–2847 in Canada; 02/ 9353–9000 in Australia; 09/526–2847 in New Zealand; 0870/ 606–0100 in the U.K.; www.avis.com). **Budget** (tel. 800/527– 0700; 0870/156–5656 in the U.K.; www.budget.com). **Dollar** (tel. 800/800–4000; 0124/622–0111 in the U.K.; where it's affiliated with Sixt; 02/9223–1444 in Australia; www.dollar.com). **Hertz** (tel. 800/654–3131; 800/263–0600 in Canada; 020/8897– 2072 in the U.K.; 02/9669–2444 in Australia; 09/256–8690 in New Zealand; www.hertz.com). **National Car Rental** (tel. 800/ 227–7368; 020/8680–4800 in the U.K.; www.nationalcar.com).

INSURANCE

When driving a rented car you are generally responsible for any damage to or loss of the vehicle. You may also be liable for any property damage or personal injury that you may cause while driving. Before you rent, see what coverage you already have under the terms of your personal auto-insurance policy and credit cards.

For about $15 to $20 a day, rental companies sell protection, known as a collision- or loss-damage waiver (CDW or LDW), that eliminates your liability for damage to the car; it's always optional and should never be automatically added to your bill. In most states you don't need a CDW if you have personal auto insurance or other liability insurance. However, **make sure you have enough coverage to pay for the car.** If you do not have auto insurance or an umbrella policy that covers damage to third parties, purchasing liability insurance and a CDW or LDW is highly recommended.

REQUIREMENTS AND RESTRICTIONS

In Washington you must be 25 to rent a car, although some companies allow employees of major corporations to rent at a younger age.

Car Travel

A car is often a drawback in Washington. Traffic is horrendous, especially at rush hours, and driving is often confusing, with many lanes and some entire streets changing direction suddenly during rush hour. Even longtime residents carry maps in their cars to help navigate confusing traffic circles and randomly arranged one-way streets. The traffic lights stymie some visitors; most lights don't hang down over the middle of the streets but stand at the sides of intersections.

EMERGENCY SERVICES

Dial 911 to report accidents on the road and to reach police, the highway patrol, or the fire department. For police non-emergencies, dial 311.

➤CONTACTS: U.S. Park Police (tel. 202/619–7300).

LAY OF THE LAND

Interstate 95 skirts D.C. as part of the Beltway, the six- to eight-lane highway that encircles the city. The eastern half of the Beltway is labeled both I–95 and I–495; the western half is just I–495. If you are coming from the south, take I–95 to I–395 and cross the 14th Street Bridge to 14th Street in the District. From the north, stay on I–95 south. Take the exit to Washington, which will place you onto the Baltimore–Washington (B-W) Parkway heading south. The B-W Parkway will turn into New York Avenue, taking you into downtown Washington, D.C.

Interstate 66 approaches the city from the southwest. You can get downtown by taking I–66 across the Theodore Roosevelt Bridge to Constitution Avenue.

Interstate 270 approaches Washington from the northwest before hitting I–495. To get downtown, take I–495 east to Connecticut Avenue south, toward Chevy Chase.

PARKING

Parking in Washington is an adventure; the police are quick to tow away or immobilize with a "boot" any vehicle parked illegally. (If you find you've been towed from a city street, call the Department of Motor Vehicles at tel. 202/727–5000 or log on to www.dmv.washingtonde.gov.) Most of the outlying, suburban Metro stations have parking lots, though these fill quickly with city-bound commuters. If you plan to park in one of these lots, arrive early, armed with lots of quarters.

Private parking lots downtown often charge around $5 an hour and $20 a day. There's free, three-hour parking around the Mall on Jefferson, Madison, and Ohio drives, though these spots are almost always filled. You can park free—in some spots all day— in parking areas off Ohio Drive near the Jefferson Memorial and south of the Lincoln Memorial on Ohio Drive and West Basin Drive in West Potomac Park.

RULES OF THE ROAD

Unless otherwise indicated by a sign, right turns at red lights are allowed in D.C. All passengers are required to wear a seat belt. Infants up to 1 year of age and under 20 pounds must be strapped into a rear-facing car seat in the back seat. Children both over age 1 and weighing 20 to 40 pounds must also use a car seat in the back seat, though it can face the front. Children cannot sit in the front seat of a car until they are at least 4 years old and weigh over 80 pounds.

During rush hour (6–9 AM and 4–7 PM), HOV (high-occupancy vehicles) lanes on I–395 and I–95 are reserved for cars with three or more persons. All the lanes of I–66 inside the beltway are reserved for cars carrying two or more during rush hour, as are some of the lanes on the Dulles Toll Road and on I–270. Radar detectors are illegal in Washington, D.C. and Virginia.

Emergencies

1–800–DOCTORS is a referral service that locates doctors, dentists, and urgent-care clinics in the greater Washington area. The D.C. Dental Society operates a referral line weekdays from 8 to 4.

➤**DOCTORS AND DENTISTS: 1–800–DOCTORS** (tel. 800/362–8677). **D.C. Dental Society** (tel. 202/547–7615).

➤**EMERGENCY SERVICES:** Dial 911 for **police, fire,** or **ambulance** in an emergency.

➤**HOSPITALS: Children's National Medical Center** (111 Michigan Ave. NW, tel. 202/884–5000). **George Washington University Hospital** (901 23rd St. NW, tel. 202/715–4911 emergencies only; 202/715–4000 non-emergencies). **Georgetown University Medical Center** (3800 Reservoir Rd. NW, tel. 202/784–2000). **Washington Hospital Center** (110 Irving St. NW, tel. 202/877–7000).

➤**24-HOUR PHARMACIES: CVS Pharmacy** (14th St. and Vermont Ave. NW on Thomas Circle, tel. 202/628–0720; 7 Dupont Circle NW, tel. 202/785–1466).

Guidebooks

Plan well and you won't be sorry. Guidebooks are excellent tools—and you can take them with you. You may want to check out pocket-size *Citypack Washington, D.C.,* which includes a foldout map; *Flashmaps Washington, D.C.,* with full-color theme maps; and Fodor's CITYGUIDE *Washington, D.C.*, for residents. All are available at on-line retailers and bookstores everywhere.

Metro Travel

The WMATA provides bus and subway service in the District and in the Maryland and Virginia suburbs. The Metro, opened in 1976, is one of the country's cleanest and safest subway systems.

DISCOUNT PASSES

For $5 you can buy a pass that allows unlimited trips for one day. It's good all day on weekends, holidays, and after 9:30 AM on weekdays. Passes are available at Metro stations and at many hotels, banks, and Safeway and Giant grocery stores.

FARES AND SCHEDULES

Trains generally run Monday through Thursday 5:30 AM–midnight, Friday and Saturday 8 AM–2 AM, and Sunday 8 AM–midnight. On Friday and Saturday, some train service ends slightly before 2 AM, so you should plan to arrive at least 10 minutes before the last train is scheduled to leave. During the weekday rush hours (5:30–9:30 AM and 3–7 PM), trains come along every six minutes. At other times and on weekends and holidays, trains run about every 12–15 minutes. The base fare is $1.10; the actual price you pay depends on the time of day and the distance traveled. Children under age five ride free when accompanied by a paying passenger, and there is a maximum of two children per paying adult.

Buy your ticket at the Farecard machines; they accept coins and crisp $1, $5, $10, or $20 bills. If the machine spits your bill back out at you, try folding and unfolding it lengthwise before asking a native for help. The Farecard should be inserted into the turnstile to enter the platform. Make sure you **hang onto the card**—you'll need it to exit at your destination.

Some Washingtonians report that the Farecard's magnetic strip interferes with the strips on ATM cards and credit cards, so **keep the cards separated in your pocket or wallet.**

➤**SUBWAY INFORMATION: Washington Metropolitan Area Transit Authority** (WMATA; tel. 202/637–7000; 202/628–8973 or 202/638–3780 TDD).

Money Matters

Washington is an expensive city, one that's comparable to New York. On the other hand, most attractions, including most of the museums, are free.

A cup of coffee in D.C. costs $1 at a diner or $4 at an upscale café; a sandwich will set you back $4.50–$7. Taxi rides cost upward of $5 depending on your destination.

Prices throughout this guide are given for adults. Substantially reduced fees are almost always available for children, students, and senior citizens. For information on taxes, *see* Taxes.

ATMS

Most ATMs in the Washington, D.C., area are linked to national networks that let you withdraw money from your checking account or take a cash advance from your credit card account for an additional fee. ATMs can be found at most banks, in many grocery stores, and in some major tourist attractions. For more information on ATM locations that can be accessed with your particular account, call the phone number found on the back of your ATM or debit card.

CREDIT CARDS

Throughout this guide, the following abbreviations are used: **AE,** American Express; **D,** Discover; **DC,** Diners Club; **MC,** MasterCard; and **V,** Visa.

Safety

D.C. is a fairly safe city, but as with any metropolitan area it's best to be alert and aware. Tourist areas and train stations are heavily patrolled by the city's numerous police affiliations. At night, stay in highly populated areas, and avoid dark streets and alleys. Panhandlers can be aggressive and may respond with verbal insults, but are otherwise usually harmless. If someone threatens you with violence for money, it's best to hand it over without a fight and seek police help later.

Sightseeing Tours

BICYCLE TOURS

Bike the Sites Tours has knowledgeable guides leading daily tours of 55 Washington landmarks; these tours are geared to the occasional exerciser. Bicycles, helmets, snacks, and water bottles are included. Prices are $40 for adults; $30 for children 12 and under. The national Adventure Cycling Association offers regional tours.

➤CONTACTS: **Adventure Cycling Association** (tel. 800/755–2453, www.adventurecycling.org). **Bike the Sites Tours** (tel. 202/966–8662, www.bikethesites.com).

BOAT TOURS

The enclosed boat called the *Dandy* cruises up the Potomac to Georgetown. Lunch cruises board weekdays starting at 10:30 AM and weekends starting at 11:30 AM. Dinner cruises board daily at 6:30 PM. Prices are $30.50–$38 for lunch and $61.50–$74.50 for dinner.

D.C. Ducks offers 90-minute tours in converted World War II amphibious vehicles from March through October. After an hour-long road tour of prominent sights, the tour moves from land to water, as the vehicle is piloted into the waters of the

Potomac for a 30-minute boat's-eye view of the city. Tickets are $25 for adults and $13 for children.

Odyssey III, a long, sleek vessel specially built to fit under the Potomac's bridges, departs from the Gangplank Marina at 6th and Water streets SW. Lunch, dinner, or Saturday and Sunday brunch cruises are among the options. Prices start at $35 and go up to $86. This upscale, glass-enclosed vessel serves elegant food; jackets are requested for men at dinner.

➤**CONTACTS: D.C. Ducks** (tel. 202/832–9800, www.historictours. com). *Odyssey* III (600 Water St. SW, tel. 202/488–6010, www.odysseycruises.com).

BUS TOURS

All About Town, Inc. has half-day, all-day, two-day, and twilight bus tours that drive by some sights and stop at others. Tours leave from various downtown locations and hotels. An all-day tour costs $36.

Gray Line has a four-hour tour of Washington, Embassy Row, and Arlington National Cemetery that leaves Union Station at 8:30 AM (late June 25–late October) and 2 PM (year-round) adults $28, children $14.

➤**CONTACTS: All About Town, Inc.** (tel. 301/856–5556, www. allabouttowntours.webatonce.com). **Gray Line** (tel. 301/386–8300, www.graylinedc.com).

ORIENTATION TOURS

Old Town Trolley Tours, orange-and-green motorized trolleys, take in the main downtown sights and also foray into Georgetown and the upper northwest. Tickets are $24. Tourmobile buses, authorized by the National Park Service, make 25 stops at more than 40 historical sites between the Capitol and Arlington National Cemetery. Tickets are $18 ($8 for children ages 3–11).

➤**CONTACTS: Old Town Trolley Tours** (tel. 202/832–9800, www.trolleytours.com). **Tourmobile** (tel. 202/554–5100, www. tourmobile.com).

PRIVATE GUIDES
Private tours can be arranged through the Guide Service of Washington and A Tour de Force. Sonny Odom offers custom photography tours.

➤**CONTACTS: Guide Service of Washington** (733 15th St. NW, Suite 1040, Washington, DC 20005, tel. 202/628–2842, www. dctourguides.com). **Sonny Odom** (2420F S. Walter Reed Dr., Arlington, VA 22206, tel. 703/379–1633, www.sonnyodom. photoreflect.com). **A Tour de Force** (Box 2782, Washington, DC 20013, tel. 703/525–2948, www.atourdeforce.com).

SPECIAL-INTEREST TOURS
Special tours of some government buildings can be arranged through your representative's or senator's office. Limited numbers of these so-called VIP tickets are available, so **plan up to six months in advance of your trip.**

Gross National Product's Scandal Tours last 75 to 90 minutes and head to some of Washington's seamier locales. Tours leave from the Pavilion at the Old Post Office Building on Saturday at 1 PM (April 1 through Labor Day only). The cost is $30 per person; reservations are required.

➤**CONTACTS: Bureau of Engraving and Printing** (14th and C Sts. SW, tel. 202/874–3188, www.bep.treas.gov). **Goodwill Embassy Tour** (tel. 202/636–4225, www.dcgoodwill.com). **Old Executive Office Building** (Pennsylvania Ave. and 17th St. NW, tel. 202/395–5895). **Gross National Product's Scandal Tours** (tel. 202/783–7212, www.gnpcomedy.com). **State Department Diplomatic Reception Rooms** (23rd and C Sts. NW, tel. 202/647–3241; 202/736–4474 TDD). **Voice of America** (330 Independence Ave. SW, tel. 202/619–3919, www.voa.gov).

Washington, D.C., Post Office (Brentwood Rd. NE between Rhode Island and New York Aves., tel. 202/636–2148). **The Washington Post** (1150 15th St. NW, tel. 202/334–7969, www. washingtonpost.com).

WALKING TOURS

Guided walks and bus tours of neighborhoods in Washington are routinely offered by the Smithsonian Resident Associates Program; advance tickets are required. Tour D.C. specializes in walking tours of Georgetown and Dupont Circle, covering historical topics such as the Civil War and the underground railroad and featuring the Kennedys' Georgetown. Guided Walking Tours of D.C. leads anecdotal history tours of Georgetown, Adams-Morgan, Capitol Hill, and the White House.

The Black History National Recreation Trail links a group of sights illustrating aspects of African-American history in Washington, from slavery days to the New Deal. A brochure outlining the trail is available from the National Park Service. Capital Entertainment Services also offers tours focusing on African-American history.

►**CONTACTS: Capital Entertainment Services** (3633 18th St. NE, Washington, DC 20018, tel. 202/636–9203, www. washington-dc-tours.com). **Guided Walking Tours of D.C.** (9009 Paddock La., Potomac, MD 20854, tel. 301/294–9514, www.dcsightseeing.com). **National Park Service** (1100 Ohio Dr. SW, Washington, DC 20242, tel. 202/619–7222, www.nps.gov). **Smithsonian Resident Associates Program** (tel. 202/357–3030, www.smithsonianassociates.org). **Tour D.C.** (1912 Glen Ross Rd., Silver Spring, MD 20910, tel. 301/588–8999, www.tourdc.com).

Taxis

Taxis in the District are not metered; they operate instead on a zone system. **Before you set off, ask your cab driver how much the fare will be.** The basic single rate for traveling within one zone is $4. There is an extra $1.50 charge for each additional passenger and a $1 surcharge during the 7–9:30 AM and 4–6:30 PM rush hours. Bulky suitcases are charged at a higher rate, and a $1.50 surcharge is tacked on when you phone for a cab. Maryland and Virginia taxis are metered but are not allowed to take passengers between points in D.C.

➤TAXI COMPANIES: Diamond Cab (tel. 202/332–6200). Taxi Transportation (tel. 202/398–0505) is an affiliation of 14 cab companies. Yellow Cab (tel. 202/544–1212).

Train Travel to and from Washington, D.C.

More than 80 trains a day arrive at Washington, D.C.'s Union Station. Acela, Amtrak's high-speed service, travels from D.C. to New York in 2½ hours and from D.C. to Boston in 6½ hours.

FARES AND SCHEDULES

Amtrak tickets and reservations are available at Amtrak stations, by telephone, through travel agents, or on-line. Amtrak schedule and fare information can be found at Union Station as well as on-line.

➤TRAIN INFORMATION: Acela (tel. 800/872–7245). Amtrak (tel. 800/872–7245, www.amtrak.com). MARC (tel. 800/325–7245, www.mtamaryland.com). Union Station (50 Massachusetts Ave. NE; tel. 202/371–9441, www.unionstationdc.com). Washington Metropolitan Area Transit Authority (WMATA; tel. 202/637–7000; 202/638–3780 or 202/628–8973 TDD, www.wmata.com).

RESERVATIONS

Amtrak has both reserved and unreserved trains available. If you plan to travel during peak times, such as a Friday night or near a holiday, you'll need to get a reservation and a ticket in advance. Some trains at nonpeak times are unreserved, with seats assigned on a first-come, first-served basis.

Travel Agencies

A good travel agent puts your needs first. Look for an agency that has been in business at least five years, emphasizes customer service, and has someone on staff who specializes in your destination. In addition, **make sure the agency belongs to a professional trade organization.** The American Society of Travel Agents (ASTA)—the largest and most influential in the field with more than 24,000 members in some 140 countries—maintains and enforces a strict code of ethics and will step in to help mediate any agent-client disputes involving ASTA members if necessary. ASTA (whose motto is "Without a travel agent, you're on your own") also maintains a Web site that includes a directory of agents.

➤**LOCAL AGENT REFERRALS: American Society of Travel Agents** (ASTA; 1101 King St., Suite 200, Alexandria, VA 22314, tel. 800/965–2782 24-hr hot line, fax 703/739–3268, www. astanet.com). **Association of British Travel Agents** (68–71 Newman St., London W1T 3AH, tel. 020/7637–2444, fax 020/ 7637–0713, www.abtanet.com). **Association of Canadian Travel Agents** (130 Albert St., Suite 1705, Ottawa, Ontario K1P 5G4, tel. 613/237–3657, fax 613/237–7052, www.acta.ca). **Australian Federation of Travel Agents** (Level 3, 309 Pitt St., Sydney, NSW 2000, tel. 02/9264–3299, fax 02/9264–1085, www. afta.com.au). **Travel Agents' Association of New Zealand** (Level 5, Tourism and Travel House, 79 Boulcott St., Box 1888, Wellington 6001, tel. 04/499–0104, fax 04/499–0827, www. taanz.org.nz).

Visitor Information

The Washington, D.C., Convention and Tourism Corporation offers a free, 128-page publication full of sightseeing tips, maps, and contacts. The Washington MTA publishes a metro and bus-system guide.

The National Portrait Gallery and the Smithsonian American Art Museum are closed for renovations through 2005. All Smithsonian museums and the National Zoo are open every day of the year except Christmas; admission is free.

➤TOURIST INFORMATION: D.C. Chamber of Commerce Visitor Center (Reagan Bldg., 1300 Pennsylvania Ave. NW, Suite 309, Washington, DC 20004, tel. 202/328–4748, www.dcvisit.com). Washington, D.C., Convention and Tourism Corporation (1212 New York Ave. NW, Suite 600, Washington, DC 20005, tel. 202/789–7000 or 800/422–8644, www.washington.org). Washington MTA (tel. 202/637–7000, www.metroopensdoors.com).

Web Sites

Do check out the World Wide Web when planning your trip. You'll find everything from weather forecasts to virtual tours of famous cities. Be sure to visit Fodors.com (www.fodors.com), a complete travel-planning site. You can research prices and book plane tickets, hotel rooms, rental cars, vacation packages, and more. In addition, you can post your pressing questions in the Travel Talk section. Other planning tools include a currency converter and weather reports, and there are loads of links to travel resources.

First Gov (www.firstgov.gov) is a directory for national, state, and local government sites. The Web site for the Library of Congress (www.cweb.loc.gov) covers current and upcoming exhibitions, visitor information, and vast, fascinating on-line exhibits. The National Register of Historic Places (www.cr.nps.gov/NR travel/wash) has a site with maps, photos, and information that takes you beyond the obvious destinations. The nation's largest museum, The Smithsonian (www.si.edu), provides a comprehensive guide to all things Smithsonian. The Washington CityPaper (www.washingtoncitypaper.com) site is a nifty and selective guide to the best of D.C.'s happenings. The Washingtonian (www.washingtonian.com) has an on-line version of its magazine, with upcoming events, restaurant reviews, and more.

When to Go

Washington has two delightful seasons: spring and autumn. In spring, the city's ornamental fruit trees are budding, and its many gardens are in bloom. By autumn, most of the summer crowds have left and you can enjoy the sights in peace. Summers can be uncomfortably hot and humid. Winter weather is often bitter, with a handful of modest snowstorms that somehow bring this southern city to a standstill. When lawmakers break for recess (at Thanksgiving, Christmas, Easter, July 4, the entire month of August, and other holiday periods), the city seems a little less vibrant.

CLIMATE

What follows are the average daily maximum and minimum temperatures for Washington.

Jan.	47F	8C	May	76F	24C	Sept.	79F	26C
	34	− 1		58	14		61	16
Feb.	47F	8C	June	85F	29C	Oct.	70F	21C
	31	− 1		65	18		52	11
Mar.	56F	13C	July	88F	31C	Nov.	56F	13C
	38	3		70	21		41	5
Apr.	67F	19C	Aug.	86F	30C	Dec.	47F	8C
	47	8		68	20		32	0

FORECASTS: Weather Channel Connection (tel. 900/932–8437), 95¢ per minute from a Touch-Tone phone.

index

211

Fodor's
Key to the Guides

America's guidebook leader publishes guides for every kind of
traveler. Check out our many series and find your perfect match.

Fodor's Gold Guides

America's favorite travel-guide series offers the most detailed insider
reviews of hotels, restaurants, and attractions in all price ranges, plus
great background information, smart tips, and useful maps.

Fodor's Road Guide USA

Big guides for a big country—the most comprehensive guides to
America's roads, packed with places to stay, eat, and play across the
U.S.A. Just right for road warriors, family vacationers, and cross-
country trekkers.

COMPASS AMERICAN GUIDES

Stunning guides from top local writers and photographers, with
gorgeous photos, literary excerpts, and colorful anecdotes. A must-
have for culture mavens, history buffs, and new residents.

Fodor's CITYPACKS

Concise city coverage with a foldout map. The right choice for urban
travelers who want everything under one cover.

Fodor's EXPLORING GUIDES

Hundreds of color photos bring your destination to life. Lively stories
lend insight into the culture, history, and people.

Fodor's POCKET GUIDES

For travelers who need only the essentials. The best of Fodor's in pocket-
size packages for just $9.95.

Fodor's To Go
Credit-card–size, magnetized color microguides that fit in the palm of your hand—perfect for "stealth" travelers or as gifts.

Fodor's FLASHMAPS
Every resident's map guide. Sixty easy-to-follow maps of public transit, parks, museums, zip codes, and more.

Fodor's CITYGUIDES
Sourcebooks for living in the city: thousands of in-the-know listings for restaurants, shops, sports, nightlife, and other city resources.

Fodor's AROUND THE CITY WITH KIDS
68 great ideas for family days, recommended by resident parents. Perfect for exploring in your own backyard or on the road.

Fodor's ESCAPES
Fill your trip with once-in-a-lifetime experiences, from ballooning in Chianti to overnighting in the Moroccan desert. These full-color dream books point the way.

Fodor's FYI
Get tips from the pros on planning the perfect trip. Learn how to pack, fly hassle-free, plan a honeymoon or cruise, stay healthy on the road, and travel with your baby.

Fodor's Languages for Travelers
Practice the local language before hitting the road. Available in phrase books, cassette sets, and CD sets.

Karen Brown's Guides
Engaging guides to the most charming inns and B&Bs in the U.S.A. and Europe, with easy-to-follow inn-to-inn itineraries.

Baedeker's Guides
Comprehensive guides, trusted since 1829, packed with A–Z reviews and star ratings.

FODOR'S POCKET WASHINGTON, D.C.

EDITORS: Shannon Kelly, John Rambow

Editorial Contributors: Susanna M. Carey, Maureen Graney, Kristi Devlin, Robin Dougherty, Satu Hummasti, Karyn-Siobhan Robinson, Christine Swiac

Editorial Production: Kristin Milavec

Maps: David Lindroth, *cartographer*; Bob Blake and Rebecca Baer, *map editors*

Design: Fabrizio La Rocca, *creative director*; Tigist Getachew, *art director*; Jolie Novak, *senior picture editor*; Melanie Marin, *photo editor*

Production/Manufacturing: Yexenia (Jessie) Markland

Cover Photo (Lincoln Memorial): Catherine Karnow/Corbis

Twelfth Edition

ISBN 1–4000–1112–4

ISSN 1094–4052

IMPORTANT TIP

Although all prices, opening times, and other details in this book are based on information supplied to us at press time, changes occur all the time in the travel world, and Fodor's cannot accept responsibility for facts that become outdated or for inadvertent errors or omissions. So **always confirm information when it matters**, especially if you're making a detour to visit a specific place.

SPECIAL SALES

Fodor's Travel Publications are available at special discounts for bulk purchases for sales promotions or premiums. Special editions, including personalized covers, excerpts of existing guides, and corporate imprints, can be created in large quantities for special needs. For more information, contact your local bookseller or write to Special Markets, Fodor's Travel Publications, 1745 Broadway, New York, New York 10019. Inquiries from Canada should be directed to your local Canadian bookseller or sent to Random House of Canada, Ltd., Marketing Department, 2775 Matheson Boulevard East, Mississauga, Ontario L4W 4P7. Inquiries from the United Kingdom should be sent to Fodor's Travel Publications, 20 Vauxhall Bridge Road, London SW1V 2SA, England.

PRINTED IN THE UNITED STATES OF AMERICA

10 9 8 7 6 5 4 3 2 1